Trust No One

The Ultimate Guide to Zero Trust Security"

By

Mark David

Table of contents

Chapter 1

The Rise of Zero Trust

Introduction to Cybersecurity Paradigms

In the early days of cybersecurity, the dominant strategy was perimeter-based security. This approach, often referred to as the "castle-and-moat" model, relied on a strong, centralized defense that protected the network from external threats. The idea was simple: create a secure perimeter around the organization's resources, and once inside, users and devices were trusted by default. Firewalls, intrusion detection systems, and other technologies were deployed to guard the perimeter, assuming that anything inside the network was safe.

However, as technology evolved, so did the threat landscape. The rise of cloud computing, mobile devices, and remote work fundamentally changed the way businesses operate. The traditional perimeter became increasingly porous, with data, applications, and users moving outside the secure confines of the corporate network. This shift exposed a critical flaw in the perimeter-based approach: once an attacker breached the perimeter, they could move laterally within the network with little resistance.

Recognizing these limitations, cybersecurity experts began to explore new strategies that could better address the complexities of modern IT environments. This search for a more robust and flexible security model eventually led to the development of the Zero Trust framework.

The Concept of Zero Trust

Zero Trust is a security model that challenges the assumptions of traditional perimeter-based security. At its core, Zero Trust operates on the principle of "never trust, always verify." Unlike the traditional model, where trust is granted by default once inside the network, Zero Trust assumes that threats could come from anywhere—inside or outside the network. As a result, every user, device, and network component is considered untrustworthy until proven otherwise.

The concept of Zero Trust was first introduced by John Kindervag, a Forrester Research analyst, in 2010. Kindervag observed that the increasing sophistication of cyber threats and the shift towards more distributed IT environments required a new approach to security. He proposed that organizations should eliminate the notion of a trusted internal network and instead focus on securing individual resources and ensuring that only authorized users and devices can access them.

Zero Trust is built on several key principles:

1. **Least Privilege Access:** Users and devices should be granted the minimum level of access necessary to perform their functions. This reduces the potential impact of a breach, as attackers are limited in what they can access.

2. **Micro-Segmentation:** The network is divided into smaller, isolated segments, each with its own security controls. This prevents lateral movement within the network and contains breaches to a limited area.

3. **Continuous Verification:** Trust is not a one-time event but a continuous process. Users and devices are constantly monitored and re-authenticated to ensure that they remain trustworthy.

4. **Multi-Factor Authentication (MFA):** MFA requires users to provide multiple forms of identification before they can access resources, adding an additional layer of security.

5. **Comprehensive Logging and Monitoring:** All network activity is logged and monitored to detect and respond to suspicious behavior in real-time.

The Evolution of Zero Trust

While the Zero Trust model was conceptualized in 2010, its adoption was initially slow. Many organizations were reluctant to abandon their existing security architectures, which were deeply ingrained in their operations. However, several key developments over the past decade have accelerated the adoption of Zero Trust:

1. **The Rise of Cloud Computing:** As organizations moved their workloads to the cloud, the traditional network perimeter began to dissolve. Cloud environments require a different

approach to security, one that can handle the dynamic and distributed nature of cloud-based resources. Zero Trust provides a framework for securing cloud environments by focusing on individual workloads rather than the network perimeter.

2. **The Increase in Remote Work:** The COVID-19 pandemic forced many organizations to adopt remote work on a massive scale. This sudden shift exposed the vulnerabilities of perimeter-based security, as employees accessed corporate resources from a variety of locations and devices. Zero Trust became a crucial strategy for securing remote work environments, ensuring that only authorized users could access

sensitive data and applications, regardless of their location.

3. **The Growing Sophistication of Cyber Threats:** Cyber threats have become more advanced and targeted, with attackers using techniques like phishing, ransomware, and supply chain attacks to infiltrate networks. Traditional security measures are often insufficient to defend against these threats. Zero Trust provides a more resilient defense by assuming that attackers may already be inside the network and focusing on limiting their ability to cause harm.

4. **Regulatory and Compliance Requirements:** Governments and

regulatory bodies have begun to recognize the importance of Zero Trust in securing critical infrastructure and protecting sensitive data. Compliance frameworks like the Cybersecurity Maturity Model Certification (CMMC) and the European Union's General Data Protection Regulation (GDPR) have incorporated Zero Trust principles, encouraging organizations to adopt this model to meet regulatory requirements.

Key Technologies Enabling Zero Trust

Several technologies have emerged as enablers of the Zero Trust model. These technologies help organizations implement the core principles of Zero

Trust and create a more secure environment:

1. **Identity and Access Management (IAM):** IAM solutions play a central role in Zero Trust by managing user identities and controlling access to resources. IAM systems enforce policies that determine who can access what, under what conditions, and with what level of privilege.

2. **Multi-Factor Authentication (MFA):** MFA requires users to provide multiple forms of verification before accessing resources. This reduces the likelihood of unauthorized access, even if a user's credentials are compromised.

3. **Software-Defined Perimeter (SDP):** SDP technology creates a dynamic and secure connection between users and resources, regardless of their location. It uses identity-based access controls to ensure that only authorized users can connect to the network.

4. **Micro-Segmentation:** Micro-segmentation solutions divide the network into smaller segments, each with its own security policies. This prevents attackers from moving laterally within the network and limits the potential impact of a breach.

5. **Security Information and Event Management (SIEM):** SIEM systems collect and analyze data from across the

network to detect and respond to security incidents in real time. In a Zero Trust environment, SIEM plays a crucial role in monitoring activity and ensuring that users and devices remain trustworthy.

The Business Case for Zero Trust

Adopting Zero Trust requires a significant investment of time and resources, but the benefits far outweigh the costs. Organizations that implement Zero Trust can achieve:

1. **Enhanced Security:** Zero Trust provides a more robust defense against modern cyber threats by assuming that attackers are already inside the network

and focusing on limiting their ability to cause harm.

2. **Reduced Risk of Breaches:** By enforcing least privilege access and micro-segmentation, Zero Trust reduces the risk of a breach and limits the potential damage if a breach does occur.

3. **Improved Compliance:** Zero Trust helps organizations meet regulatory requirements by ensuring that sensitive data is protected and that access is tightly controlled.

4. **Increased Flexibility:** Zero Trust is well-suited to modern IT environments, including cloud computing, remote work, and mobile devices. It provides a

flexible and scalable security framework that can adapt to changing business needs.

The Future of Zero Trust

As the digital landscape continues to evolve, Zero Trust is poised to become the new standard for cybersecurity. Organizations across all industries are recognizing the limitations of traditional security models and embracing Zero Trust as a more effective approach to protecting their assets. In the coming years, we can expect to see continued innovation in Zero Trust technologies, as well as broader adoption across both private and public sectors.

The rise of Zero Trust marks a fundamental shift in the way we think about cybersecurity. By moving away from the outdated notion of a secure perimeter and adopting a more dynamic and flexible security model, organizations can better protect themselves against the ever-changing threat landscape.

By understanding the principles and technologies that underpin Zero Trust, organizations can better prepare themselves for the future and ensure that they are ready to defend against the threats of tomorrow.

Chapter 2

Building Blocks of Zero Trust Architecture

Introduction to Zero Trust Architecture

Zero Trust Architecture (ZTA) is a cybersecurity model designed to address the challenges posed by modern IT environments, where traditional perimeter-based security approaches are insufficient. Zero Trust operates on the principle of "never trust, always verify," meaning that no entity—whether inside or outside the network—should be trusted by default. Every request for access is treated as though it could be malicious, and verification is required at every stage.

ZTA provides a comprehensive approach to securing an organization's data, applications, and infrastructure. It involves a combination of technologies, policies, and processes that work together to minimize the risk of unauthorized access and data breaches. In this chapter, we will explore the fundamental building blocks of Zero Trust Architecture, including identity and access management, device security, network segmentation, and continuous monitoring.

1. Identity and Access Management (IAM)

1.1. Role of Identity in Zero Trust:

At the core of Zero Trust is the concept of identity as the new perimeter. In traditional models, the network boundary served as the primary security control. However, with the rise of cloud computing, mobile devices, and remote work, the network perimeter has become increasingly blurred. In a Zero Trust environment, identity becomes the key to determining access rights. Every user, device, and service must be uniquely identifiable, and their access rights must be carefully managed and enforced.

1.2. Identity Verification:

Identity verification involves confirming that the entity requesting access is who they claim to be. This is typically achieved through multi-factor authentication (MFA), which requires users to provide multiple forms of verification, such as a password, a fingerprint, or a one-time code sent to their mobile device. MFA is a critical component of Zero Trust because it significantly reduces the likelihood of unauthorized access, even if a user's credentials are compromised.

1.3. Role-Based Access Control (RBAC) and Attribute-Based Access Control (ABAC):

Role-Based Access Control (RBAC) and Attribute-Based Access Control (ABAC) are two key methods for managing access rights within a Zero Trust environment. RBAC assigns access rights based on a user's role within the organization, while ABAC uses a combination of attributes—such as user identity, device type, and location—to determine access. These methods ensure that users have access only to the resources they need to perform their duties, reducing the risk of lateral movement by attackers.

1.4. Identity Federation and Single Sign-On (SSO):

In a Zero Trust Architecture, identity federation and Single Sign-On (SSO) are often used to streamline the authentication process across multiple systems and platforms. Identity federation allows organizations to extend their identity management capabilities to external partners, enabling secure collaboration without compromising security. SSO simplifies the user experience by allowing users to access multiple applications with a single set of credentials, while still enforcing the principles of Zero Trust.

2. Device Security

2.1. Device Identification and Posture Assessment:

Just as the identity of users must be verified, so too must the identity of devices. Device identification ensures that only known, authorized devices can access the network. This involves checking the device's unique identifiers, such as its MAC address, and ensuring that it meets the organization's security standards. Posture assessment goes a step further by evaluating the device's current state—such as its operating system version, patch level, and security settings—to determine if it meets the security requirements for accessing sensitive resources.

2.2. Endpoint Detection and Response (EDR):

Endpoint Detection and Response (EDR) solutions play a critical role in Zero Trust by continuously monitoring devices for signs of compromise. EDR tools collect and analyze data from endpoints—such as laptops, smartphones, and IoT devices—in real-time, allowing security teams to detect and respond to threats quickly. In a Zero Trust environment, EDR is essential for maintaining visibility into device activity and ensuring that compromised devices are identified and isolated before they can cause harm.

2.3. Mobile Device Management (MDM):

With the increasing use of mobile devices in the workplace, Mobile Device Management (MDM) has become an important component of Zero Trust. MDM solutions enable organizations to enforce security policies on mobile devices, such as requiring encryption, enforcing password policies, and remotely wiping devices that are lost or stolen. MDM also allows for the segmentation of work and personal data on mobile devices, ensuring that sensitive corporate data remains protected even on employee-owned devices.

2.4. Device Authentication and Authorization:

Device authentication is the process of verifying that a device is authorized to access the network. This can be achieved through various methods, such as certificates, tokens, or cryptographic keys. Once a device is authenticated, its access rights must be carefully controlled, ensuring that it can only access the resources for which it is authorized. This principle of least privilege is central to Zero Trust, as it minimizes the potential attack surface and limits the damage that can be done by compromised devices.

3. Network Segmentation and Micro-Segmentation

3.1. Traditional Network Segmentation:

Network segmentation involves dividing a network into smaller, isolated segments, each with its own security controls. In traditional network security models, segmentation was often achieved through the use of VLANs, firewalls, and access control lists (ACLs). These controls limited the ability of attackers to move laterally within the network, reducing the risk of widespread breaches.

3.2. Micro-Segmentation:

Micro-segmentation takes the concept of network segmentation to the next level by creating even smaller, more granular segments—down to the level of individual workloads or applications. This approach enables organizations to enforce security policies at a more detailed level, ensuring that only authorized entities can communicate with each other. Micro-segmentation is often implemented using software-defined networking (SDN) technologies, which allow for dynamic and flexible control over network traffic.

3.3. East-West Traffic Control:

In a traditional network, most security controls are focused on North-South traffic—that is, traffic entering and leaving the network. However, in a Zero Trust environment, it is equally important to control East-West traffic, or traffic moving laterally within the network. Micro-segmentation allows for the monitoring and control of East-West traffic, ensuring that unauthorized communication between network segments is prevented. This is particularly important for detecting and preventing lateral movement by attackers who have already breached the perimeter.

3.4. Software-Defined Perimeter (SDP):

A Software-Defined Perimeter (SDP) is a security framework that dynamically creates secure connections between users and resources based on identity. SDP is often used in conjunction with micro-segmentation to create a Zero Trust environment. It provides a flexible and scalable way to control access to resources, ensuring that only authorized users can connect to the network, regardless of their location or device.

4. Continuous Monitoring and Threat Detection

4.1. Continuous Monitoring:

In a Zero Trust Architecture, security is not a one-time event but an ongoing process. Continuous monitoring involves the real-time collection and analysis of data from across the network to detect and respond to threats as they arise. This data includes network traffic, user behavior, and system logs, among other things. Continuous monitoring allows organizations to maintain visibility into their environment and quickly identify any signs of compromise.

4.2. Security Information and Event Management (SIEM):

Security Information and Event Management (SIEM) systems are critical to continuous monitoring in a Zero Trust environment. SIEM solutions collect and correlate data from multiple sources, providing a centralized view of security events across the network. They use advanced analytics and machine learning to detect anomalies and identify potential threats. In a Zero Trust environment, SIEM plays a key role in ensuring that all activity is monitored and that any suspicious behavior is immediately investigated.

4.3. Behavioral Analytics and Anomaly Detection:

Behavioral analytics involves the use of machine learning and statistical models to analyze user and device behavior and detect deviations from normal patterns. Anomaly detection is a key component of this process, as it helps identify potential security incidents that might otherwise go unnoticed. In a Zero Trust Architecture, behavioral analytics is essential for detecting insider threats and compromised accounts, as it allows organizations to identify unusual activity that could indicate malicious intent.

4.4. Automated Threat Response:

As cyber threats become more sophisticated, the need for rapid response has become increasingly important. Automated threat response involves the use of artificial intelligence (AI) and machine learning to automatically detect and respond to security incidents. In a Zero Trust environment, automated threat response can help organizations quickly contain and mitigate threats before they can cause significant damage. This might include actions such as isolating compromised devices, blocking malicious traffic, or revoking access privileges.

5. Data Security and Encryption

5.1. Data Classification and Access Control:

Data security is a critical component of Zero Trust, as it ensures that sensitive information is protected from unauthorized access. Data classification involves categorizing data based on its sensitivity and implementing access controls that restrict access to only those who need it. In a Zero Trust environment, data access is tightly controlled, with policies that enforce the principle of least privilege and ensure that sensitive data is only accessible to authorized users.

5.2. Encryption:

Encryption is a fundamental aspect of data security in a Zero Trust Architecture. It involves the use of cryptographic algorithms to protect data both at rest (stored data) and in transit (data being transmitted over the network). Encryption ensures that even if data is intercepted or accessed by unauthorized parties, it cannot be read or used without the appropriate decryption keys. In a Zero Trust environment, encryption is applied consistently across all data, regardless of its location or state.

5.3. Data Loss Prevention (DLP):

Data Loss Prevention (DLP) solutions are essential in a Zero Trust environment, providing mechanisms to monitor and control the movement of sensitive data. DLP tools prevent unauthorized access, use, or transmission of data by enforcing policies that dictate how data can be used, where it can be stored, and who can access it. DLP solutions are often integrated with other security technologies, such as SIEM and IAM, to ensure comprehensive protection. By identifying and blocking potential data exfiltration attempts, DLP helps organizations maintain compliance with regulations and protect their intellectual property and customer data.

5.4. Secure Data Access Policies:

Zero Trust Architecture requires stringent data access policies that go beyond traditional access control. These policies define who can access specific data, under what circumstances, and from which devices or locations. Access controls must be dynamic, adapting to the context of the request, such as the user's role, device security posture, and the sensitivity of the data. Zero Trust demands that data access is continuously verified, with real-time monitoring to detect and respond to any anomalies that may indicate a security breach.

6. Application Security

6.1. Securing Applications in a Zero Trust Environment:

Applications are a primary target for cyber attackers, making application security a critical component of Zero Trust Architecture. Zero Trust demands that every application be treated as a potential point of vulnerability. This involves implementing security measures at every stage of the application lifecycle, from development to deployment and operation.

6.2. DevSecOps and Continuous Integration/Continuous Deployment (CI/CD):

DevSecOps integrates security into the development process, ensuring that security best practices are followed from the earliest stages of application development. In a Zero Trust environment, DevSecOps practices are critical for identifying and mitigating security risks before applications are deployed. Continuous

Integration/Continuous Deployment (CI/CD) pipelines automate the process of integrating security checks into the development workflow, enabling organizations to deploy secure applications quickly and efficiently.

6.3. Runtime Application Self-Protection (RASP):

Runtime Application Self-Protection (RASP) is a security technology that integrates directly into applications to monitor and protect them during runtime. RASP tools detect and block malicious activity in real-time, providing an additional layer of defense against application-level attacks. In a Zero Trust Architecture, RASP ensures that applications remain secure even if other security controls are bypassed.

6.4. Secure API Management:

Application Programming Interfaces (APIs) are a key component of modern applications, enabling different systems to communicate and share data. However, APIs can also introduce security risks if not properly managed. In a Zero Trust environment, secure API management is crucial for controlling access to applications and data. This involves enforcing strict authentication and authorization policies for APIs, as well as monitoring and logging API activity to detect and respond to potential threats.

7. Visibility and Analytics

7.1. Importance of Visibility in Zero Trust:

Visibility is a cornerstone of Zero Trust Architecture. To effectively enforce Zero Trust principles, organizations must have comprehensive visibility into all activities within their environment. This includes monitoring user behavior, network traffic, device activity, and application usage. Visibility is essential for identifying potential security incidents, understanding the context of access requests, and enforcing security policies.

7.2. Network Traffic Analysis:

Network traffic analysis involves monitoring and analyzing the flow of data across the network to detect anomalies that may indicate a security breach. In a Zero Trust environment, network traffic analysis is used to identify unauthorized access attempts, lateral movement, and data exfiltration. Advanced analytics tools can correlate data from multiple sources to provide a complete picture of network activity and identify potential threats in real-time.

7.3. User and Entity Behavior Analytics (UEBA):

User and Entity Behavior Analytics (UEBA) is a key technology in Zero Trust Architecture, providing the ability to detect unusual behavior that may indicate a security threat. UEBA tools use machine learning algorithms to establish a baseline of normal behavior for users, devices, and entities within the network. When behavior deviates from this baseline, the system generates alerts for further investigation. UEBA is particularly effective at detecting insider threats and compromised accounts, as it can identify subtle changes in behavior that might otherwise go unnoticed.

7.4. Security Orchestration, Automation, and Response (SOAR):

Security Orchestration, Automation, and Response (SOAR) platforms are used to automate the response to security incidents in a Zero Trust environment.

SOAR tools integrate with other security technologies, such as SIEM and EDR, to automatically respond to threats based on predefined playbooks. This enables organizations to respond to security incidents more quickly and efficiently, reducing the time it takes to contain and mitigate threats.

8. Policy Enforcement

8.1. Centralized Policy Management:

Centralized policy management is essential for enforcing Zero Trust principles across an organization's entire IT environment. This involves creating and maintaining security policies that define how access is granted, how data is protected, and how threats are mitigated. Centralized policy management tools allow organizations to enforce these policies consistently across all users, devices, applications, and networks, regardless of their location.

8.2. Dynamic Access Control Policies:

In a Zero Trust Architecture, access control policies must be dynamic and context-aware. This means that access decisions are based on a combination of factors, including user identity, device posture, network location, and the sensitivity of the requested resource. Dynamic access control policies allow organizations to adapt to changing conditions in real-time, ensuring that access is granted only when it is safe to do so.

8.3. Policy Enforcement Points (PEPs):

Policy Enforcement Points (PEPs) are the components of Zero Trust Architecture responsible for enforcing security policies. PEPs are distributed throughout the network and are responsible for verifying access requests and ensuring that they comply with the organization's security policies. PEPs can be implemented as hardware appliances, software agents, or cloud-based services, depending on the organization's needs.

8.4. Policy Decision Points (PDPs):

Policy Decision Points (PDPs) are responsible for making access control decisions in a Zero Trust environment. When a user or device requests access to a resource, the PEP forwards the request to the PDP, which evaluates the request against the organization's security policies. The PDP then returns a decision to the PEP, which either grants or denies access based on the decision. PDPs play a critical role in ensuring that access control decisions are made consistently and in accordance with the organization's security policies.

9. Implementation Strategies for Zero Trust Architecture

9.1. Assessing the Current Security Posture:

Before implementing Zero Trust Architecture, organizations must assess their current security posture to identify gaps and areas for improvement. This involves conducting a thorough security audit to evaluate existing security controls, identify vulnerabilities, and understand the current threat landscape. The results of this assessment will inform the development of a Zero Trust implementation plan.

9.2. Phased Implementation Approach:

Implementing Zero Trust Architecture is a complex process that requires careful planning and execution. A phased implementation approach allows organizations to gradually introduce Zero Trust principles and technologies, reducing the risk of disruption to business operations. This approach typically involves prioritizing critical assets and high-risk areas, and then expanding the implementation to cover the entire IT environment.

9.3. Integrating with Existing Security Infrastructure:

Zero Trust Architecture does not require organizations to abandon their existing security infrastructure. Instead, it can be integrated with existing tools and technologies, such as firewalls, SIEM, IAM, and EDR, to enhance security and provide a more comprehensive defense. Organizations should evaluate their existing security infrastructure to determine how it can be leveraged to support Zero Trust principles.

9.4. Employee Training and Awareness:

A successful Zero Trust implementation requires more than just technology—it also requires a cultural shift within the organization. Employees must be trained on the principles of Zero Trust and understand their role in maintaining a secure environment. This includes training on best practices for identity and access management, data protection, and recognizing and responding to security threats. Ongoing training and awareness programs are essential for maintaining a strong security posture in a Zero Trust environment.

Conclusion

Zero Trust Architecture represents a fundamental shift in the way organizations approach cybersecurity. By focusing on identity, device security, network segmentation, continuous monitoring, and data protection, Zero Trust provides a comprehensive framework for defending against modern cyber threats. Implementing Zero Trust is a complex process that requires careful planning, integration with existing security infrastructure, and a commitment to continuous improvement. However, the benefits of Zero Trust—enhanced security, reduced risk of breaches, and improved compliance—make it a critical component of any organization's cybersecurity strategy.

As cyber threats continue to evolve, Zero Trust Architecture will play an increasingly important role in protecting organizations' most valuable assets. By adopting the building blocks of Zero Trust, organizations can create a more resilient and adaptive security posture that is capable of withstanding the challenges of the modern threat landscape.

Chapter 3:

Identity, Access, and Authentication in Zero Trust

In the modern digital landscape, the principles of Identity, Access, and Authentication (IAA) have become foundational to cybersecurity, especially within a Zero Trust Architecture (ZTA). Traditional security models relied on the assumption that entities inside the network could be trusted, while those outside could not. However, the explosion of cloud services, mobile devices, remote work, and sophisticated cyber threats have rendered these assumptions obsolete. Zero Trust challenges the conventional perimeter-based security model by asserting that no entity—whether inside or outside the network—should be trusted by default. Instead, security must be enforced at every level, beginning with the very core of user and device identity.

This chapter delves deeply into the core aspects of IAA within Zero Trust, exploring how identity is established, how access is controlled, and how authentication ensures that only legitimate users and devices gain access to resources.

1. Identity: The New Perimeter

1.1. The Importance of Identity in Zero Trust

In a Zero Trust model, identity becomes the new perimeter, replacing the traditional network boundary. This shift recognizes that security cannot be limited to network edges; instead, it must be integrated into every interaction between users, devices, applications, and data. Every entity, whether human or machine, must have a verifiable identity before it can interact with any part of the system.

1.2. Identity Providers and Federation

Identity Providers (IdPs) play a crucial role in Zero Trust by managing the identities of users and devices. IdPs authenticate entities and provide identity tokens that can be used to gain access to resources. These tokens are essential for enforcing Zero Trust principles, as they allow for the verification of identity at every stage of an interaction.

Identity federation extends this capability by allowing different organizations to share and trust identities across boundaries. For example, a company can trust the identity of a user from a partner organization if both use federated identity services. This is particularly important in a Zero Trust environment where collaboration across organizational boundaries is common, yet security must remain tight.

1.3. Identity Governance and Administration (IGA)

Identity Governance and Administration (IGA) is the framework for managing and controlling digital identities and their access rights across an organization. IGA includes identity lifecycle management, role management, and access certification processes, ensuring that users have the appropriate level of access at all times. In a Zero Trust model, IGA is critical for ensuring that identities are correctly managed, with access rights continuously aligned to the principle of least privilege.

IGA solutions typically include features such as automated provisioning and deprovisioning of user accounts, role-based access control (RBAC), and periodic access reviews. These tools help maintain the integrity of the identity ecosystem, ensuring that only authorized individuals have access to critical resources.

2. Access Control: Enforcing Least Privilege

2.1. Principle of Least Privilege

The principle of least privilege (PoLP) is a fundamental tenet of Zero Trust. It dictates that users and devices should only have the minimum access necessary to perform their functions. By minimizing access rights, PoLP reduces the potential attack surface and limits the damage that can be caused by compromised accounts or insider threats.

In a Zero Trust environment, access control must be granular and dynamic. It requires continuous assessment of whether a user or device should retain access based on their current role, context, and behavior. This dynamic nature is a departure from traditional static access controls, which often grant broad, unchanging access rights that can be exploited by attackers.

2.2. Role-Based Access Control (RBAC) and Attribute-Based Access Control (ABAC)

RBAC and ABAC are two predominant access control models used in Zero Trust Architecture:

- **Role-Based Access Control (RBAC):** RBAC assigns permissions based on the roles that users have within an organization. For example, an employee in the finance department may have access to accounting software but not to the development environment. RBAC simplifies management by grouping permissions under roles, but it can be rigid and may not accommodate all scenarios, especially in dynamic environments.

- Attribute-Based Access Control (ABAC): ABAC, on the other hand, is more flexible and dynamic. It evaluates access requests based on a variety of attributes, such as the user's identity, device posture, time of access, and sensitivity of the data. For example, ABAC can enforce policies like "Allow access to financial records only during business hours from a company-issued device." This level of granularity is crucial in a Zero Trust environment where context-aware security is paramount.

2.3. Context-Aware Access

In a Zero Trust environment, access decisions must be made based on context, rather than static rules. Context-aware access takes into account a variety of factors, such as the location of the user, the device they are using, their current behavior, and the sensitivity of the data they are trying to access. For example, a user accessing a sensitive document from an unfamiliar location might be required to undergo additional verification steps before being granted access.

Context-aware access is often implemented through policies that define the conditions under which access can be granted. These policies must be continuously evaluated and updated to reflect the current threat landscape and organizational needs.

2.4. Dynamic Access Controls and Just-In-Time Access

Dynamic access controls are a key feature of Zero Trust, allowing for real-time adjustment of access rights based on changing circumstances. This is particularly important in environments where user roles and responsibilities change frequently, or where the security posture of a device can fluctuate.

Just-In-Time (JIT) access is a concept where users are granted access to resources only for a specific task and for a limited time. Once the task is completed, access is revoked. This approach minimizes the risk of unauthorized access by ensuring that users only have the necessary permissions when they are actively working on a task.

3. Authentication: Verifying Identity

3.1. Multi-Factor Authentication (MFA)

Multi-Factor Authentication (MFA) is a cornerstone of Zero Trust security. It requires users to present multiple forms of verification before access is granted. Typically, MFA combines something the user knows (a password), something the user has (a security token or mobile device), and something the user is (biometrics like a fingerprint or facial recognition).

MFA significantly enhances security by making it much harder for attackers to gain unauthorized access, even if they have obtained the user's password. In a Zero Trust model, MFA is often required for all access attempts, especially when accessing sensitive resources or performing privileged actions.

3.2. Passwordless Authentication

Passwordless authentication is an emerging trend in Zero Trust, aimed at addressing the vulnerabilities associated with traditional passwords. Passwordless methods rely on alternatives such as biometrics, hardware tokens, or mobile devices for authentication. This approach not only improves security but also enhances user experience by eliminating the need for users to remember and manage passwords.

Examples of passwordless authentication include:

- **Biometric Authentication:** Uses physical characteristics such as fingerprints, facial recognition, or voice recognition to verify identity.
- **Hardware Tokens:** Devices like YubiKeys that generate unique codes or use public-key cryptography to authenticate users.
- **Push Notifications:** Sends a notification to a user's mobile device, which they approve to complete the authentication process.

Passwordless authentication aligns well with Zero Trust principles by providing stronger, more user-friendly security mechanisms that reduce the reliance on vulnerable passwords.

3.3. Continuous Authentication

Continuous authentication is a concept where user identity is continuously verified throughout the duration of a session, rather than just at the initial login. This approach is essential in Zero Trust environments, where trust must be constantly re-evaluated.

Continuous authentication can involve monitoring user behavior, such as typing patterns, mouse movements, and application usage, to detect anomalies that might indicate a compromised session. If an anomaly is detected, the system can prompt the user for re-authentication or terminate the session altogether.

3.4. Adaptive Authentication

Adaptive authentication takes the concept of context-aware security further by adjusting the authentication requirements based on the risk level of the access request. For example, a user logging in from a trusted device at a usual time might only be asked for a password, while the same user logging in from an unfamiliar device or location might be required to provide additional verification factors.

Adaptive authentication uses risk-based algorithms to evaluate the context of the access attempt and apply the appropriate level of security. This ensures that security is strong enough to protect sensitive resources, but not so burdensome that it hinders legitimate users.

4. The Role of Identity in Zero Trust Networking

4.1. Identity-Centric Security

In Zero Trust, identity is not just a user credential but the linchpin of the entire security framework. Identity-centric security means that every interaction within the network is mediated and controlled based on verified identities. This applies to not only users but also devices, applications, and APIs.

Identity-centric security strategies ensure that only verified and authorized identities can access the network, and that their actions within the network are continuously monitored and controlled. This approach drastically reduces the risk of unauthorized access and lateral movement by attackers.

4.2. Zero Trust Network Access (ZTNA)

Zero Trust Network Access (ZTNA) is a technology that enforces Zero Trust principles by providing secure, granular access to applications and resources based on identity and context. Unlike traditional VPNs, which provide broad access to network segments, ZTNA solutions only grant access to specific applications or services based on the identity of the user and the security posture of their device.

ZTNA solutions typically involve the use of identity-aware proxies that authenticate and authorize users before allowing them to access applications. These proxies enforce policies that determine what resources a user can access, based on their role, location, device, and other contextual factors.

4.3. Privileged Access Management (PAM)

Privileged Access Management (PAM) is a critical component in the Zero Trust framework because it focuses on securing, managing, and monitoring access to high-level or "privileged" accounts within an organization. These accounts typically have broader access to systems and data, making them prime targets for cyber attackers. The compromise of a privileged account can lead to catastrophic breaches, as attackers can use these accounts to move laterally across the network, escalate privileges further, and access sensitive data.

In Zero Trust Architecture, PAM solutions enforce strict controls over privileged accounts, including:

- **Just-In-Time (JIT) Access:** This approach ensures that privileged access is granted only when necessary and for a limited time. After the task is completed, the elevated access is automatically revoked, thereby reducing the window of opportunity for misuse.

- **Session Monitoring and Recording:** PAM tools often include capabilities to monitor and record all activities performed by privileged users. This provides an audit trail that can be reviewed for suspicious activities and ensures that users are held accountable for their actions.

- **Credential Management:** PAM solutions also manage the credentials of privileged accounts, ensuring that passwords are complex, regularly rotated, and stored securely. Some advanced PAM systems can even eliminate the need for passwords altogether by using passwordless authentication methods, which enhances security.

- **Least Privilege Enforcement:** Even within privileged accounts, PAM systems enforce the principle of least privilege by ensuring that users only have access to the resources they need to perform their job. This minimizes the potential impact of a compromised account.

By integrating PAM into a Zero Trust Architecture, organizations can significantly reduce the risk associated with privileged accounts and ensure that even their most powerful users are subject to stringent security controls.

5. Identity and Access Management (IAM) in Zero Trust

5.1. Centralized IAM Systems

In a Zero Trust model, centralized Identity and Access Management (IAM) systems are essential for managing and enforcing security policies across the organization. These systems provide a single point of control for managing user identities, access rights, and authentication processes. IAM systems are responsible for ensuring that every user and device is authenticated and authorized before gaining access to any resource.

Centralized IAM systems offer several advantages in a Zero Trust environment:

- **Consistency:** A centralized approach ensures that security policies are applied consistently across all users and devices, regardless of their location or role.

- **Scalability:** As organizations grow, centralized IAM systems can scale to accommodate new users, devices, and applications, while maintaining strong security controls.

- **Integration:** Modern IAM solutions integrate with other security tools, such as SIEM, PAM, and UEBA, providing a comprehensive security posture that aligns with Zero Trust principles.

5.2. Identity Lifecycle Management

Identity lifecycle management refers to the processes and technologies used to manage the entire lifecycle of user identities, from creation to termination.

In a Zero Trust environment, it is crucial that identity lifecycle management is automated and tightly controlled to ensure that access rights are always aligned with the user's current role and responsibilities.

The key stages of identity lifecycle management include:

- **Provisioning:** Automatically creating user accounts and assigning appropriate access rights when a new employee joins the organization.

- **Deprovisioning:** Ensuring that access rights are promptly revoked when an employee leaves the organization or changes roles.

- **Access Reviews:** Regularly reviewing and certifying that users have the correct access rights for their current roles.

- **Role Management:** Defining and managing roles within the organization, ensuring that access rights are based on the principle of least privilege.

5.3. Integration with Cloud Services

As organizations increasingly move to cloud-based services, IAM systems must integrate seamlessly with cloud environments to enforce Zero Trust principles. This includes managing identities and access rights across a hybrid environment that spans on-premises and cloud-based resources.

Cloud-based IAM solutions offer several benefits, such as:

- **Elasticity:** The ability to scale up or down based on the organization's needs, without requiring significant investment in on-premises infrastructure.

- **Global Reach:** Providing consistent access management for users regardless of their geographic location.

- **Advanced Security Features:** Cloud IAM solutions often come with built-in security features such as AI-driven threat detection, which helps organizations detect and respond to potential security incidents in real-time.

6. Challenges and Considerations in Implementing IAA in Zero Trust

6.1. User Experience vs. Security

One of the primary challenges in implementing robust IAA mechanisms in Zero Trust is balancing security with user experience. While Zero Trust requires stringent authentication and access controls, these measures can sometimes be perceived as burdensome by users, potentially leading to resistance or workarounds.

To address this, organizations must focus on implementing security measures that are both effective and user-friendly. For example, adaptive authentication and passwordless methods can enhance security while simplifying the user experience. Additionally, educating users about the importance of these security measures and how they protect the organization can help foster a security-conscious culture.

6.2. Legacy Systems Integration

Many organizations still rely on legacy systems that may not natively support modern IAM or Zero Trust principles. Integrating these systems into a Zero

Trust environment can be challenging, as they may lack the necessary interfaces for centralized identity management, access control, and continuous monitoring.

Organizations must assess their legacy systems to determine whether they can be updated or replaced to support Zero Trust. In some cases, it may be necessary to implement compensating controls, such as network segmentation and additional monitoring, to mitigate the risks associated with legacy systems.

6.3. Scalability and Performance

As organizations grow and their IT environments become more complex, ensuring that IAA mechanisms scale effectively is critical. IAM systems, in particular, must be able to handle large volumes of authentication requests without compromising performance.

To achieve this, organizations should invest in IAM solutions that are designed for scalability and high availability. Additionally, using cloud-based IAM services can help distribute the load and ensure consistent performance across global operations.

6.4. Regulatory Compliance

Compliance with data protection regulations such as GDPR, CCPA, and HIPAA is a significant consideration when implementing Zero Trust IAA mechanisms. These regulations often require organizations to implement specific identity and access controls, as well as to ensure that user data is protected and accessible only to authorized individuals.

Organizations must ensure that their IAM and PAM systems support compliance requirements, including data encryption, access logging, and regular audits. Failure to comply with these regulations can result in severe penalties and reputational damage.

Conclusion

Identity, Access, and Authentication (IAA) are the cornerstones of Zero Trust Architecture, ensuring that every user, device, and application is continuously verified and monitored. By implementing robust IAA mechanisms, organizations can significantly reduce the risk of unauthorized access, data breaches, and other cyber threats.

In a Zero Trust environment, identity becomes the new perimeter, and access is granted based on the principle of least privilege. Authentication is continuous and context-aware, ensuring that only legitimate users and devices can interact with sensitive resources. While there are challenges to implementing these mechanisms, the benefits of enhanced security, reduced risk, and improved compliance make it a critical investment for any organization seeking to protect its digital assets in an increasingly complex and hostile threat landscape.

As organizations continue to adopt Zero Trust principles, the focus on Identity, Access, and Authentication will only become more important. By staying ahead of emerging threats and continuously improving their IAA strategies, organizations can build a resilient security posture that is capable of withstanding the evolving challenges of the digital age.

Chapter 4

Network Security and
Micro-Segmentation

Network security has always been a critical aspect of cybersecurity, serving as the first line of defense against threats to an organization's digital assets. Traditionally, network security focused on protecting the perimeter, assuming that threats originated outside the network. However, the evolving cyber threat landscape, characterized by sophisticated attacks and insider threats, has rendered perimeter-based defenses insufficient. In the context of Zero Trust Architecture (ZTA), the concept of network security is redefined to focus on securing the network from the inside out, rather than relying solely on perimeter defenses.

A key component of this approach is micro-segmentation, a technique that divides the network into smaller, more manageable segments, each with its own set of security controls. Micro-segmentation plays a crucial role in the Zero Trust model by limiting lateral movement within the network, ensuring that even if a threat actor breaches one segment, they cannot easily access other parts of the network.

This chapter provides a comprehensive overview of network security in the context of Zero Trust, with a particular focus on the role of micro-segmentation.

It covers the principles, techniques, and technologies that underpin network security in a Zero Trust environment, offering practical insights into how organizations can protect their networks from both external and internal threats.

1. The Evolution of Network Security

1.1. Traditional Network Security Models

Traditional network security models have long relied on the concept of a "trusted" internal network protected by a robust perimeter, typically enforced by firewalls, intrusion detection systems (IDS), and intrusion prevention systems

(IPS). The assumption was that threats would primarily originate from outside the organization, so the focus was on keeping external attackers at bay while allowing trusted users within the network to operate freely.

However, this model has several limitations:

- **Implicit Trust:** Once inside the network, users and devices are often granted broad access without rigorous checks, creating opportunities for attackers to move laterally and escalate privileges.

- **Static Defenses:** Traditional defenses are often static, unable to adapt quickly to emerging threats or changes in the network environment.

- **Complexity and Visibility:** As networks have grown in size and complexity, it has become increasingly difficult to maintain visibility and control over all network traffic, leading to blind spots where threats can go undetected.

1.2. The Shift to Zero Trust Network Security

The shift towards Zero Trust has fundamentally changed the approach to network security. Rather than relying on a secure perimeter, Zero Trust assumes that no entity—whether inside or outside the network—can be trusted by default. Every user, device, and application must be continuously authenticated, authorized, and monitored.

Key principles of Zero Trust network security include:

- **No Implicit Trust:** Every access request is treated as potentially malicious, regardless of the request's origin within the network.

- **Least Privilege:** Users and devices are granted the minimum level of access required to perform their tasks, reducing the potential attack surface.

- Continuous Monitoring: Network activity is continuously monitored for signs of anomalous behavior, and access rights are dynamically adjusted based on real-time risk assessments.

2. Micro-Segmentation: The Cornerstone of Zero Trust Network Security

2.1. Understanding Micro-Segmentation

Micro-segmentation is a network security technique that divides a network into small, isolated segments, each protected by its own set of security controls. Unlike traditional network segmentation, which might separate

networks based on broad categories
(e.g., internal vs. external, production
vs. development), micro-segmentation
goes further by creating granular
segments down to the level of individual
workloads, applications, or even user
groups.

Each segment can have its own security
policies, ensuring that access is tightly
controlled and limited to only those
entities that require it. This approach is
highly effective in preventing lateral
movement, a common tactic used by
attackers once they gain a foothold in
the network.

2.2.   Implementing
Micro-Segmentation

Implementing micro-segmentation requires a detailed understanding of the network's architecture, including the flow of data between applications, users, and devices. The process typically involves:

- **Asset and Data Flow Mapping:** Before implementing micro-segmentation, it's crucial to map out the network's assets and understand how data flows between them. This helps in defining the appropriate segments and security policies.

- **Defining Security Policies:** Each segment must have its own set of security policies, based on the principle of least privilege. Policies should define who can access the segment, under what conditions, and what actions they can perform.

- **Enforcing Segmentation:** Micro-segmentation can be enforced using various technologies, such as software-defined networking (SDN), network virtualization, or host-based firewalls. The chosen technology should allow for dynamic enforcement of security policies, adapting to changes in the network environment.

- **Continuous Monitoring and Adjustment:** Once micro-segmentation is in place, it's essential to continuously monitor network traffic for signs of policy violations or suspicious behavior. Segments and policies should be regularly reviewed and adjusted based on the evolving threat landscape.

2.3. Micro-Segmentation Technologies

Several technologies can be used to implement micro-segmentation:

- **Software-Defined Networking (SDN):** SDN decouples the control plane from the data plane, allowing network administrators to dynamically control traffic flows and enforce segmentation policies centrally. This flexibility is ideal for implementing micro-segmentation in complex, distributed environments.

- Network Virtualization: Network virtualization technologies, such as VMware NSX, allow for the creation of virtual networks that are isolated from each other, even when running on the same physical infrastructure. This enables granular segmentation and control over network traffic.

- Host-Based Firewalls: Host-based firewalls can enforce micro-segmentation at the individual workload or application level, ensuring that only authorized traffic is allowed to reach sensitive resources.

- Cloud-Native Security Solutions:
Cloud environments often provide built-in micro-segmentation capabilities, such as AWS Security Groups or Azure Network Security Groups, which allow for the isolation of workloads within cloud environments.

3. Benefits of Micro-Segmentation in Zero Trust

3.1. Limiting Lateral Movement

One of the primary benefits of micro-segmentation is its ability to limit lateral movement within the network. Even if an attacker successfully breaches one segment, they are unable to move freely across the network, as each segment requires separate authentication and authorization. This significantly reduces the potential impact of a breach.

3.2. Granular Control and Visibility

Micro-segmentation provides organizations with granular control over network traffic, allowing them to enforce security policies at a much more detailed level than traditional segmentation. This leads to better visibility into network activity and makes it easier to detect and respond to threats.

3.3. Improved Compliance

Many regulatory frameworks require organizations to implement strong access controls and to segment sensitive data from the rest of the network. Micro-segmentation helps organizations meet these requirements by ensuring that sensitive resources are isolated and protected according to the principle of least privilege.

3.4. Flexibility and Scalability

Micro-segmentation is highly flexible and can be scaled to accommodate changes in the network environment. New segments can be created as needed, and security policies can be dynamically adjusted to reflect changes in risk levels.

This makes micro-segmentation particularly well-suited to modern, dynamic IT environments, such as cloud-based infrastructures.

4. Challenges of Micro-Segmentation

4.1. Complexity and Management Overhead

Implementing micro-segmentation can be complex, especially in large, distributed networks. Managing a large number of segments and associated policies can create significant overhead, requiring specialized tools and expertise.

4.2. Performance Considerations

Micro-segmentation can introduce performance overhead, particularly if segments are implemented using host-based firewalls or other resource-intensive technologies. Organizations must carefully plan their segmentation strategy to minimize performance impacts while ensuring robust security.

4.3. Integration with Legacy Systems

Legacy systems may not support modern micro-segmentation techniques, making it challenging to integrate them into a segmented network. In some cases, organizations may need to implement compensating controls or consider upgrading legacy systems to support micro-segmentation.

4.4. Continuous Policy Management

Micro-segmentation requires continuous management and adjustment of security policies to remain effective. This can be resource-intensive, particularly in environments where roles, responsibilities, and network configurations are constantly changing.

5. Network Security Tools and Technologies in Zero Trust

5.1. Next-Generation Firewalls (NGFWs)

Next-Generation Firewalls (NGFWs) are a critical component of network security in a Zero Trust environment. Unlike traditional firewalls, NGFWs offer advanced features such as deep packet inspection, intrusion prevention, and application-layer filtering. NGFWs can enforce micro-segmentation policies by inspecting traffic at a granular level and ensuring that only authorized communications are allowed between segments.

5.2. Intrusion Detection and Prevention Systems (IDPS)

Intrusion Detection and Prevention Systems (IDPS) play a crucial role in Zero Trust network security by continuously monitoring network traffic for signs of malicious activity. IDPS can be integrated with micro-segmentation to detect and respond to threats within individual segments, providing an additional layer of defense against lateral movement.

5.3. Network Access Control (NAC)

Network Access Control (NAC) solutions enforce Zero Trust principles by controlling which devices are allowed to connect to the network and under what conditions. NAC can enforce micro-segmentation by ensuring that only devices with the appropriate security posture are allowed to access specific segments.

5.4. Security Information and Event Management (SIEM)

SIEM systems are integral to network security in a Zero Trust environment due to their ability to collect and analyze security events in real-time from multiple sources, including network devices, servers, and applications. By correlating data across these sources, SIEM systems can identify potential security incidents that might otherwise go unnoticed. In the context of micro-segmentation, SIEMs provide valuable insights into the interactions between segments, helping to detect anomalous behavior that could indicate a breach or insider threat.

SIEM systems can also be integrated with automated response mechanisms, allowing them to take immediate action in response to detected threats. For instance, if a SIEM detects unusual traffic patterns between two segments, it can automatically trigger an alert or even initiate a response, such as isolating the affected segments to prevent further spread of the threat.

5.5. Software-Defined Perimeter (SDP)

Software-Defined Perimeter (SDP) is another key technology that complements micro-segmentation in a Zero Trust network security framework. SDPs create secure, encrypted tunnels between users and the resources they need to access, effectively hiding those resources from the broader network. This reduces the attack surface and ensures that only authenticated and authorized users can access specific network segments.

An SDP solution can dynamically adapt to changes in the network environment, ensuring that access policies are enforced consistently across all segments, regardless of where the users or resources are located. This makes

SDPs particularly valuable in cloud and hybrid environments, where traditional network security controls may be difficult to implement.

5.6. Endpoint Detection and Response (EDR)

Endpoint Detection and Response (EDR) solutions are crucial for maintaining network security within a Zero Trust framework. EDR tools monitor endpoint devices (such as laptops, desktops, and mobile devices) for signs of compromise and can detect malicious activity at the device level before it has a chance to propagate through the network.

In a micro-segmented network, EDR solutions play a vital role in ensuring that each segment remains secure by continuously monitoring endpoints for threats. If a compromise is detected, EDR tools can isolate the affected endpoint from the network, preventing lateral movement to other segments.

5.7. Secure Access Service Edge (SASE)

Secure Access Service Edge (SASE) is an emerging network architecture that integrates network security functions (such as SD-WAN, secure web gateways, and cloud access security brokers) with Zero Trust principles. SASE is designed to provide secure access to applications and data, regardless of the user's location or the network they are using.

In a Zero Trust framework, SASE supports micro-segmentation by applying consistent security policies across all network traffic, whether it originates from within the corporate network or from remote users. SASE solutions can dynamically segment traffic based on identity, device posture, and other contextual factors, ensuring that security is enforced at the edge of the network.

6. Challenges in Implementing Network Security and Micro-Segmentation

6.1. Complexity of Network Environments

One of the primary challenges in implementing micro-segmentation is the complexity of modern network environments. Organizations often have a mix of legacy systems, cloud-based services, and modern applications, all of which need to be integrated into a unified segmentation strategy. This requires a deep understanding of the network's architecture, including how data flows between different systems and applications.

To address this complexity, organizations can use network mapping and visualization tools that provide a clear picture of network traffic patterns and dependencies. These tools help in designing effective micro-segmentation policies that minimize disruption while maximizing security.

6.2. Management Overhead

Managing a large number of network segments can create significant overhead for IT and security teams. Each segment requires its own set of security policies, which need to be continuously monitored and adjusted to reflect changes in the network environment. This can be resource-intensive, particularly in dynamic environments where roles, responsibilities, and applications are constantly changing.

Automation can help reduce management overhead by streamlining the process of policy creation, enforcement, and adjustment. For example, security orchestration, automation, and response (SOAR) platforms can automate many of the routine tasks associated with micro-segmentation, allowing security teams to focus on more strategic activities.

6.3. Performance Considerations

Implementing micro-segmentation can impact network performance, particularly if segments are enforced using resource-intensive technologies like host-based firewalls. This can lead to increased latency, reduced throughput, and other performance issues that may affect the user experience.

To mitigate these issues, organizations need to carefully plan their segmentation strategy, considering factors such as the placement of security controls, the sensitivity of data, and the performance characteristics of different segments. In some cases, it may be necessary to invest in additional network infrastructure or optimize existing resources to maintain performance while enforcing segmentation policies.

6.4. User Experience and Adaptation

As with any security measure, there is a potential for micro-segmentation to impact user experience, particularly if users are frequently required to authenticate and re-authenticate to access different segments. This can lead to frustration and may encourage users to seek workarounds, undermining the effectiveness of the security measures.

To minimize the impact on user experience, organizations should consider implementing adaptive authentication mechanisms that adjust the level of security required based on the user's context. For example, a user accessing a low-risk segment from a trusted device might only need to authenticate once, while access to a high-risk segment from an unknown device might require additional verification steps.

6.5. Integration with Legacy Systems

Legacy systems often lack the capabilities required to support modern network security techniques like micro-segmentation. This can create challenges when trying to integrate these systems into a segmented network, as they may not be compatible with the technologies or security policies used in other segments.

In some cases, organizations may need to implement compensating controls, such as additional monitoring or network isolation, to secure legacy systems. However, these measures are often less effective than native support for micro-segmentation, so organizations should also consider upgrading or replacing legacy systems where possible.

7. Best Practices for Network Security and Micro-Segmentation in Zero Trust

7.1. Start with a Detailed Network Inventory

Before implementing micro-segmentation, it's essential to conduct a thorough inventory of the network's assets, including all devices, applications, and data flows. This inventory provides the foundation for designing effective segmentation policies and ensures that no critical assets are overlooked.

7.2. Define Clear Segmentation Policies

Segmentation policies should be based on the principle of least privilege, ensuring that each segment is only accessible to those users and devices that require it. Policies should be well-documented, with clear rules for who can access each segment and under what conditions.

7.3. Implement Strong Monitoring and Analytics

Continuous monitoring is critical to the success of micro-segmentation in a Zero Trust environment. Organizations should implement robust monitoring and analytics tools that can detect and respond to threats in real-time. This includes monitoring traffic between segments, as well as within each segment, to ensure that security policies are being enforced effectively.

7.4. Leverage Automation

Automation can significantly reduce the complexity and management overhead associated with micro-segmentation. Organizations should leverage automation tools to streamline the process of policy creation, enforcement, and adjustment, allowing security teams to focus on more strategic activities.

7.5. Regularly Review and Update Segmentation Policies

Network environments are constantly changing, so it's essential to regularly review and update segmentation policies to reflect these changes. This includes re-evaluating the network inventory, adjusting policies based on new threats, and ensuring that segmentation remains aligned with the organization's overall security strategy.

7.6. Educate Users and Stakeholders

Finally, it's important to educate users and stakeholders about the purpose and benefits of micro-segmentation, as well as how it impacts their day-to-day activities. By fostering a culture of security awareness, organizations can reduce the likelihood of resistance or workarounds that could undermine the effectiveness of their security measures.

Conclusion

Network security and micro-segmentation are central to the Zero Trust approach, providing a robust framework for protecting an organization's digital assets in an increasingly complex and hostile cyber environment. By dividing the network into small, isolated segments, organizations can limit lateral movement, reduce the attack surface, and ensure that security policies are enforced consistently across all parts of the network.

While implementing micro-segmentation can be challenging, the benefits in terms of improved security, compliance, and visibility make it a worthwhile investment for any organization. By following best practices and leveraging the right tools and technologies, organizations can build a resilient network security posture that is capable of withstanding the evolving threats of the digital age.

Chapter 5

Data Security and Encryption Practices

In the era of digital transformation, data is often regarded as the most valuable asset for organizations. Protecting this data from unauthorized access, corruption, or theft has become a critical concern for businesses, governments, and individuals alike. The advent of sophisticated cyber threats, coupled with stringent regulatory requirements, has made data security a top priority. Central to any data security strategy is the use of encryption, a powerful tool that ensures that even if data falls into the wrong hands, it remains unreadable and unusable.

This chapter explores the essential components of data security within the Zero Trust framework, with a specific focus on encryption practices. It delves into the principles of data security, the different types of encryption, key management, and best practices for implementing robust encryption strategies. Additionally, it addresses the challenges and emerging trends in data security, providing insights into how organizations can stay ahead of evolving threats.

1. The Fundamentals of Data Security

1.1. What is Data Security?

Data security refers to the set of measures and protocols designed to protect data from unauthorized access, alterations, disclosure, or destruction. These measures encompass a wide range of strategies, including physical security, access controls, encryption, and data masking. The primary goal of data security is to ensure the confidentiality, integrity, and availability (CIA) of data, whether at rest, in transit, or in use.

- **Confidentiality:** Ensures that sensitive data is accessible only to authorized users or systems.
- **Integrity:** Guarantees that data remains accurate and unaltered during its lifecycle.

- **Availability:** Ensures that data is accessible to authorized users when needed.

1.2. The Role of Data Security in Zero Trust

In a Zero Trust model, the traditional notion of a secure perimeter is replaced with a model that assumes that no user, device, or application can be trusted by default, whether inside or outside the network. This assumption extends to data security, where Zero Trust principles dictate that all data must be protected at all times, regardless of its location or who is attempting to access it.

Zero Trust enforces strict access controls, continuous monitoring, and comprehensive encryption practices to protect data. This means that data security measures must be integrated into every layer of the network, from the endpoints and applications to the cloud and data centers.

2. Encryption: The Cornerstone of Data Security

2.1. What is Encryption?

Encryption is the process of converting plain text or data into an encoded format that can only be read by someone with the correct decryption key. This process ensures that even if data is intercepted or accessed by unauthorized individuals, it remains unintelligible.

There are two main types of encryption:

- **Symmetric Encryption:** Uses the same key for both encryption and decryption. It is generally faster but requires secure key distribution.

- **Asymmetric Encryption:** Uses a pair of keys—a public key for encryption and a private key for decryption. It is more secure for key distribution but slower compared to symmetric encryption.

2.2. The Role of Encryption in Data Security

Encryption is a fundamental element of data security in a Zero Trust environment. It protects data at all stages of its lifecycle, whether at rest (stored data), in transit (data being transmitted over networks), or in use (data being processed). By ensuring that data is encrypted, organizations can protect sensitive information from unauthorized access, even if other security measures fail.

Encryption is also a critical component of regulatory compliance, with many laws and regulations requiring organizations to encrypt sensitive data.

Examples include the General Data Protection Regulation (GDPR) in the European Union, the Health Insurance Portability and Accountability Act (HIPAA) in the United States, and the Payment Card Industry Data Security Standard (PCI DSS).

3. Types of Encryption

3.1. Symmetric Encryption

Symmetric encryption uses a single key for both encryption and decryption. The most commonly used symmetric encryption algorithms include:

- **Advanced Encryption Standard (AES):** A widely adopted encryption standard known for its speed and security. AES supports key lengths of 128, 192, and 256 bits.

- **Data Encryption Standard (DES) and Triple DES (3DES):** Once widely used, DES has largely been replaced by AES due to its shorter key length, which makes it more vulnerable to brute-force attacks. 3DES applies the DES algorithm three times to each data block, improving security.

Advantages of Symmetric Encryption:

- Fast and efficient, making it suitable for encrypting large amounts of data.

- Requires less computational power compared to asymmetric encryption.

Challenges of Symmetric Encryption:
- Key distribution and management can be complex, especially in large organizations.
- If the encryption key is compromised, all encrypted data is at risk.

3.2. Asymmetric Encryption

Asymmetric encryption uses a pair of keys—one public and one private. The public key encrypts the data, while the private key decrypts it. Common asymmetric encryption algorithms include:

- **Rivest-Shamir-Adleman (RSA):** One of the first public-key cryptosystems and still widely used for secure data transmission.

- **Elliptic Curve Cryptography (ECC):** Offers the same level of security as RSA but with shorter key lengths, making it faster and more efficient.

Advantages of Asymmetric Encryption:

- Simplifies key distribution, as the public key can be shared openly while the private key remains secure.

- Provides a higher level of security, especially for key exchange and digital signatures.

Challenges of Asymmetric Encryption:

- Slower than symmetric encryption due to the complexity of the mathematical operations involved.

- Requires more computational resources, which can be a drawback in resource-constrained environments.

3.3. Hybrid Encryption

Hybrid encryption combines the strengths of both symmetric and asymmetric encryption. Typically, asymmetric encryption is used to securely exchange a symmetric key, which is then used to encrypt the actual data. This approach leverages the speed of symmetric encryption and the security of asymmetric encryption.

Hybrid encryption is commonly used in secure communication protocols, such as Transport Layer Security (TLS) and Secure Sockets Layer (SSL), which are the foundations of secure web browsing.

4. Key Management in Encryption

4.1. The Importance of Key Management

Effective key management is crucial to the success of any encryption strategy. Key management involves generating, distributing, storing, rotating, and eventually retiring encryption keys. Poor key management practices can undermine the security of even the most robust encryption algorithms.

4.2. Key Management Practices

- **Key Generation:** Keys should be generated using strong, random processes to ensure their security. The length of the key should be sufficient to protect against brute-force attacks, with longer keys offering greater security.

- **Key Distribution:** Secure methods must be used to distribute encryption keys, particularly in symmetric encryption. Public key infrastructure (PKI) is often used to manage the distribution of asymmetric keys.

- **Key Storage:** Encryption keys should be stored securely, using hardware security modules (HSMs) or other secure storage solutions. Keys should never be hard-coded into software or stored in plain text.

- **Key Rotation:** Regularly rotating encryption keys reduces the risk of keys being compromised. Rotation should be done in a way that minimizes disruption to operations.

- **Key Revocation and Retirement:** When keys are no longer needed or are suspected to be compromised, they should be revoked and securely retired. This process should be carefully managed to avoid data loss or downtime.

4.3. Key Management Solutions

Many organizations use dedicated key management solutions (KMS) to automate and manage the lifecycle of encryption keys. These solutions can integrate with various encryption technologies and provide a centralized platform for key management, reducing the complexity and risk associated with manual key management.

5. Encryption in Data at Rest, in Transit, and in Use

5.1. Data at Rest

Data at rest refers to data that is stored on a device or within a database. Encrypting data at rest is critical to protecting it from unauthorized access, particularly in the event of physical theft or unauthorized access to storage systems.

- **Full Disk Encryption (FDE):** Encrypts the entire contents of a storage device, ensuring that all data is protected. FDE is commonly used on laptops, smartphones, and other portable devices.

- **Database Encryption:** Databases can be encrypted at the file level, column level, or using transparent data encryption (TDE), which encrypts the entire database without requiring changes to the application.

5.2. Data in Transit

Data in transit refers to data that is being transmitted over a network, whether within an organization or over the internet. Encrypting data in transit is essential to protecting it from interception and tampering.

- Transport Layer Security (TLS): TLS is the most widely used protocol for securing data in transit, particularly in web communications. It encrypts data between the client and server, preventing eavesdropping and man-in-the-middle attacks.

- Virtual Private Networks (VPNs): VPNs create secure, encrypted tunnels for transmitting data between remote locations, protecting data from being intercepted during transmission.

5.3. Data in Use

Data in use is a particularly vulnerable state because it must be decrypted and accessible to the application or system for processing, making it susceptible to attacks. Traditional encryption methods protect data at rest and in transit, but securing data in use requires more advanced techniques. Two emerging technologies—Homomorphic Encryption and Secure Multi-Party Computation (SMPC)—are paving the way for more secure data processing.

- **Homomorphic Encryption:** This encryption method allows computations to be performed on ciphertext (encrypted data) without needing to decrypt it first. The results of these computations are also in an encrypted form, which can be decrypted only by someone with the appropriate key. This means sensitive data can be processed while remaining encrypted, reducing the risk of exposure to unauthorized users. Though still in its early stages and computationally intensive, homomorphic encryption is seen as a promising solution for secure data processing in cloud environments, where sensitive data needs to be processed by third-party services.

- Secure Multi-Party Computation (SMPC): SMPC enables multiple parties to jointly compute a function over their inputs while keeping those inputs private. Each party's data is encrypted and divided into shares, which are then distributed among the participants. None of the parties can access the full data, but they can still work together to compute the desired function securely. This is particularly useful in collaborative environments where multiple entities need to share and process sensitive information without revealing their individual data, such as in financial services, healthcare, and data analytics.

These techniques are vital in Zero Trust environments where the assumption is that threats can come from anywhere, and protecting data at every stage, including while it is being processed, is essential.

6. Best Practices for Implementing Data Security and Encryption

6.1. Comprehensive Data Classification

Before implementing any data security measures, it is critical to classify data based on its sensitivity and value to the organization. Data classification involves categorizing data into different levels, such as public, internal, confidential, and restricted. This process helps determine the appropriate level of protection required for each data type, guiding encryption and access control decisions.

- Steps for Data Classification:

   - Identify Data Types: Determine the types of data being processed and stored within the organization, including personal, financial, intellectual property, and operational data.

- **Assess Sensitivity:** Evaluate the sensitivity of each data type based on regulatory requirements, business impact, and potential harm if compromised.

- **Assign Classification Levels:** Classify data into categories such as public, confidential, or highly confidential, and apply security measures accordingly.

6.2. Encryption Everywhere

Organizations should adopt an "encryption everywhere" strategy to protect data across its entire lifecycle, whether it is at rest, in transit, or in use. This approach ensures that data is protected regardless of its state or location, reducing the risk of unauthorized access or data breaches.

- **Data at Rest:** Implement full disk encryption, database encryption, and file-level encryption to protect stored data. Ensure that encryption keys are managed securely and rotated regularly.

- **Data in Transit:** Use TLS/SSL, VPNs, and secure email protocols to encrypt data as it moves across networks. Implement mutual authentication to verify the identities of communicating parties.

- **Data in Use:** Explore advanced encryption techniques like homomorphic encryption and SMPC to protect data during processing. Ensure

that access to decrypted data is strictly
controlled and monitored.

6.3. Strong Key Management Practices

Effective key management is critical to
maintaining the security of encrypted
data. Organizations must implement
robust key management practices to
generate, distribute, store, and retire
encryption keys securely.

- **Key Generation:** Use secure,
random processes to generate
encryption keys, ensuring they are
sufficiently long to resist brute-force
attacks.

- **Key Storage:** Store keys in secure locations, such as hardware security modules (HSMs), and avoid embedding keys in applications or scripts.

- **Key Rotation:** Regularly rotate encryption keys to minimize the risk of compromise. Ensure that key rotation is done in a manner that does not disrupt business operations.

- **Key Revocation:** Establish procedures for revoking and securely retiring keys that are no longer needed or suspected of being compromised.

6.4. Regular Security Audits and Penetration Testing

Regular security audits and penetration testing are essential for identifying vulnerabilities in data security practices. These assessments help organizations evaluate the effectiveness of their encryption strategies and identify areas for improvement.

- **Security Audits:** Conduct periodic audits to assess compliance with data security policies and regulatory requirements. Audits should include a review of encryption practices, key management, access controls, and data classification.

- **Penetration Testing:** Engage ethical hackers to perform penetration tests that simulate real-world attacks on the organization's encryption systems. Penetration testing helps identify weaknesses that could be exploited by attackers and provides actionable insights for enhancing security.

6.5. Employee Training and Awareness

Human error is a significant factor in data breaches, making employee training and awareness programs crucial to any data security strategy. Employees must be educated on the importance of data security and encryption, as well as best practices for protecting sensitive information.

- **Security Awareness Programs:** Implement ongoing security awareness programs that cover topics such as phishing, password management, and the proper handling of sensitive data. Use real-world scenarios and examples to reinforce key concepts.

- **Role-Based Training:** Provide specialized training for employees based on their roles and responsibilities. For example, IT staff should receive training on encryption technologies and key management, while legal and compliance teams should be educated on regulatory requirements.

6.6. Compliance with Regulations and Standards

Organizations must ensure that their data security practices comply with relevant regulations and industry standards. Compliance not only protects the organization from legal penalties but also enhances customer trust and confidence.

- **Regulatory Compliance:** Identify the regulations that apply to the organization's industry and geographic location, such as GDPR, HIPAA, or PCI DSS. Implement encryption practices that meet or exceed the requirements of these regulations.

- **Industry Standards:** Adhere to industry standards and best practices for data security and encryption, such as those outlined by the National Institute of Standards and Technology (NIST) or the International Organization for Standardization (ISO).

7. Challenges in Data Security and Encryption

7.1. Performance Impact

Encryption can have a performance impact, particularly in environments where large amounts of data are processed or transmitted. Encrypting and decrypting data requires computational resources, which can slow down systems and affect user experience.

- Mitigating Performance Issues: To mitigate performance issues, organizations can optimize their encryption algorithms and hardware. For example, using hardware-accelerated encryption can significantly reduce the performance impact. Additionally, hybrid encryption methods that combine symmetric and asymmetric encryption can balance security and performance.

7.2. Complexity of Key Management

Managing encryption keys across a large organization can be complex and challenging. The need to generate, distribute, store, rotate, and revoke keys securely requires significant resources and expertise.

- **Key Management Solutions:** Organizations can invest in key management solutions (KMS) that automate many of the processes involved in key management. KMS solutions can integrate with existing security infrastructure, reducing complexity and improving key security.

7.3. Data Sovereignty and Cloud Encryption

Data sovereignty refers to the concept that data is subject to the laws and regulations of the country in which it is located. This presents challenges for organizations that store data in the cloud, as they may need to comply with multiple jurisdictions' regulations.

- **Cloud Encryption Practices:** To address data sovereignty challenges, organizations can implement client-side encryption, where data is encrypted before it is uploaded to the cloud. This ensures that the organization retains control over the encryption keys and can comply with data protection regulations.

7.4. The Evolving Threat Landscape

The threat landscape is constantly evolving, with attackers developing new techniques to bypass encryption and other security measures. This makes it essential for organizations to stay updated on the latest threats and continuously improve their data security practices.

- Proactive Security Measures: Organizations should adopt a proactive approach to security, including threat intelligence, continuous monitoring, and regular updates to encryption protocols. By staying ahead of emerging threats, organizations can better protect their data from advanced attacks.

8. Emerging Trends in Data Security and Encryption

8.1. Quantum-Resistant Encryption

The development of quantum computing presents a significant challenge to current encryption methods. Quantum computers have the potential to break widely used encryption algorithms, such as RSA and ECC, much faster than classical computers.

- Quantum-Resistant Algorithms: In response to this threat, researchers are developing quantum-resistant encryption algorithms that can withstand attacks from quantum computers. These algorithms are still in the experimental stage, but they represent an important area of focus for future data security.

8.2. Confidential Computing

Confidential computing is an emerging technology that aims to protect data in use by isolating it within a secure enclave or trusted execution environment (TEE). This ensures that even if the underlying infrastructure is compromised, the data remains secure.

- **Applications of Confidential Computing:** Confidential computing is particularly valuable in cloud environments, where data is processed on third-party infrastructure. It enables organizations to process sensitive data without exposing it to the cloud provider or other external entities.

8.3. Data Privacy and Encryption

Data privacy concerns are driving the adoption of encryption technologies that prioritize user privacy. This includes end-to-end encryption (E2EE), which ensures that only the communicating parties can access the data, with no possibility of interception by third parties.

- **Privacy-Enhancing Technologies (PETs):** Privacy-enhancing technologies, such as differential privacy and secure computation, are being integrated with encryption to provide stronger privacy guarantees. These technologies allow organizations to analyze and share data while preserving individual privacy.

Conclusion

As the digital landscape continues to evolve, so too must the strategies and technologies used to protect sensitive data. The Zero Trust model, with its emphasis on continuous verification, least privilege access, and comprehensive encryption practices, provides a robust framework for securing data in today's complex and ever-changing threat environment.

Encryption is a key component of data security within this framework, protecting data at rest, in transit, and in use. However, encryption alone is not enough. Effective key management, regular security audits, employee training, and compliance with regulatory requirements are also essential to maintaining a strong data security posture.

Emerging technologies, such as homomorphic encryption, quantum-resistant algorithms, and confidential computing, offer new ways to enhance data security and protect against the threats of tomorrow. By staying informed about these developments and continuously improving their data security practices, organizations can better protect their most valuable asset: their data.

In summary, Chapter 5 has provided a comprehensive overview of data security and encryption practices within the context of a Zero Trust architecture. As organizations continue to face new and evolving threats, they must remain vigilant and proactive in their approach to data security. By adopting best practices, leveraging emerging technologies, and maintaining a strong commitment to protecting sensitive information, organizations can ensure that their data remains secure, even in the face of the most sophisticated cyber attacks.

Chapter 6

Monitoring, Analytics, and Threat Detection

6.1. Introduction to Monitoring and Threat Detection in Zero Trust

In a Zero Trust environment, where trust is never assumed and verification is constant, monitoring, analytics, and threat detection play crucial roles in maintaining security. The goal is not just to detect potential breaches but also to anticipate and mitigate them before they can cause harm. Unlike traditional security models that focus primarily on perimeter defenses, Zero Trust requires continuous visibility into all activities

172

within the network, including user behavior, application access, data flows, and network communications.

Monitoring and analytics in Zero Trust are closely intertwined with threat detection. Through comprehensive monitoring, data is collected, which is then analyzed using advanced analytics techniques. This analysis helps in identifying patterns, detecting anomalies, and triggering alerts for potential security incidents. In essence, monitoring and analytics serve as the eyes and ears of a Zero Trust architecture, enabling real-time detection and response to threats.

6.2. The Importance of Continuous Monitoring

Continuous monitoring is a cornerstone of Zero Trust. Given that Zero Trust operates on the assumption that threats can arise from both outside and inside the network, real-time monitoring of all activities is essential for maintaining security.

- **Network Monitoring:** Continuous network monitoring involves tracking all network traffic, including the movement of data between users, devices, and applications. This helps in detecting unauthorized access, unusual data transfers, and other suspicious activities that may indicate a security breach.

Network monitoring tools in a Zero Trust environment should provide visibility into encrypted traffic, as attackers often use encryption to hide their activities.

- Endpoint Monitoring: With the rise of remote work and BYOD (Bring Your Own Device) policies, endpoint security has become more critical than ever. Continuous monitoring of endpoints—such as laptops, smartphones, and IoT devices—helps in identifying compromised devices and preventing them from accessing sensitive resources. Endpoint Detection and Response (EDR) tools are often used in Zero Trust environments to monitor endpoint activities, detect malicious behavior, and initiate automatic responses.

- Identity and Access Monitoring: Monitoring user identities and access privileges is essential for enforcing the principle of least privilege. Continuous monitoring of authentication events, login attempts, and access requests helps in detecting compromised accounts or insider threats. Identity monitoring tools can also identify unusual behavior, such as an employee attempting to access data they don't usually interact with, which could be an early indicator of a security incident.

- Application Monitoring: In a Zero Trust architecture, applications are a prime target for attackers, as they often contain sensitive data and perform critical functions. Continuous monitoring of applications helps detect vulnerabilities, unauthorized modifications, or misuse. Application Performance Monitoring (APM) tools, coupled with security monitoring, provide insights into both the performance and security of applications.

6.3. Advanced Analytics for Threat Detection

Advanced analytics is essential for making sense of the vast amounts of data collected through continuous monitoring. In a Zero Trust environment, where threats can be sophisticated and subtle, traditional rule-based detection methods are often insufficient. Instead, organizations must leverage machine learning, behavioral analytics, and AI-driven tools to detect anomalies and predict potential security incidents.

- **Behavioral Analytics:** Behavioral analytics involves analyzing the behavior of users, devices, and applications to establish baselines of normal activity. Once these baselines are established, deviations from the norm can be detected as potential threats. For example, if a user suddenly accesses large amounts of sensitive data outside of their usual working hours, this could trigger an alert for further investigation.

- **Machine Learning and AI:** Machine learning (ML) and artificial intelligence (AI) are increasingly used in threat detection to analyze vast datasets, identify patterns, and predict potential threats. ML models can be trained on historical data to recognize the characteristics of known threats, and AI can continuously adapt and improve its detection capabilities based on new data. This allows for more accurate and timely detection of emerging threats that may not have been previously encountered.

- Threat Intelligence Integration:
Integrating threat intelligence feeds with monitoring and analytics tools enhances the ability to detect and respond to known threats. Threat intelligence provides context about emerging threats, such as indicators of compromise (IoCs), which can be used to strengthen monitoring rules and improve detection accuracy. Real-time threat intelligence enables organizations to stay ahead of evolving threats and adapt their security posture accordingly.

6.4. Automated Threat Detection and Response

Automation is a critical component of Zero Trust threat detection and response. Given the sheer volume of data generated by continuous monitoring, manual threat detection is not feasible. Automated systems can analyze data in real-time, detect threats, and initiate response actions without human intervention.

- **Security Orchestration, Automation, and Response (SOAR):** SOAR platforms are designed to automate security operations, including threat detection, incident response, and remediation. In a Zero Trust environment, SOAR tools can automatically quarantine compromised devices, block malicious IP addresses, and enforce additional authentication measures when suspicious activity is detected. Automation not only speeds up the response time but also reduces the risk of human error in critical situations.

- **Intrusion Detection and Prevention Systems (IDPS):** IDPS solutions are a key element of automated threat detection in Zero Trust. These systems monitor network traffic for signs of malicious activity and can take immediate action to block or mitigate threats. In a Zero Trust environment, IDPS tools are often integrated with other security systems, such as firewalls and endpoint protection, to provide a coordinated defense against threats.

- Incident Response Automation:
Automated incident response involves predefined workflows that are triggered when specific threats are detected. For example, if a user account is compromised, the automated response might include disabling the account, notifying the security team, and initiating an investigation. Automation ensures that incidents are addressed promptly, minimizing the potential impact on the organization.

6.5. Threat Detection Challenges in a Zero Trust Environment

While Zero Trust offers a robust security framework, implementing effective threat detection in this environment is not without challenges. These challenges include the complexity of monitoring and analyzing vast amounts of data, the risk of false positives, and the need to balance security with user experience.

- **Data Overload:** Continuous monitoring generates enormous amounts of data, making it difficult to identify relevant security events. Organizations must invest in scalable analytics platforms capable of processing and analyzing this data in real-time. Failure to do so can result in critical threats being overlooked.

- False Positives: Advanced analytics and automated systems can sometimes generate false positives, where benign activities are flagged as potential threats. High false positive rates can lead to alert fatigue among security teams, causing real threats to be missed. Organizations must fine-tune their detection algorithms and use contextual information to reduce false positives.

- Balancing Security and Usability: In a Zero Trust environment, security measures such as continuous authentication and monitoring can impact user experience. For example, frequent authentication prompts can frustrate users and hinder productivity. Organizations must strike a balance between robust security and user convenience by implementing adaptive security measures that adjust based on the level of risk.

6.6. Best Practices for Effective Monitoring and Threat Detection

To maximize the effectiveness of monitoring, analytics, and threat detection in a Zero Trust environment, organizations should follow best practices that enhance their security posture and reduce the risk of breaches.

- **Comprehensive Visibility:** Ensure that monitoring covers all aspects of the network, including endpoints, applications, and cloud services. Comprehensive visibility is essential for detecting threats across the entire attack surface.

- Contextual Awareness: Leverage contextual information, such as user roles, device types, and network locations, to enhance threat detection accuracy. Contextual awareness allows security teams to differentiate between normal and suspicious activities more effectively.

- Regular Updates and Patching: Keep all monitoring and threat detection tools up to date with the latest security patches and updates. This reduces vulnerabilities that attackers could exploit to bypass detection.

- Incident Response Planning: Develop and regularly update an incident response plan that outlines the steps to take in the event of a security breach. Ensure that the plan includes automated response workflows to minimize response times.

- Continuous Improvement: Regularly review and refine monitoring and threat detection processes based on lessons learned from previous incidents and new threat intelligence. Continuous improvement is key to staying ahead of evolving threats.

6.7. Emerging Trends in Monitoring and Threat Detection

The field of monitoring and threat detection is rapidly evolving, with new technologies and approaches emerging to address the challenges of modern cybersecurity.

- **Extended Detection and Response (XDR):** XDR is an emerging technology that integrates data from multiple security components, including endpoints, networks, and applications, into a unified platform for threat detection and response. XDR offers improved visibility and faster response times compared to traditional security solutions.

- **Deception Technology:** Deception technology involves deploying decoys and traps within the network to lure attackers and detect their activities early in the attack lifecycle. This proactive approach helps organizations identify and respond to threats before they can cause significant damage.

- **Zero Trust Network Access (ZTNA):** ZTNA is a new approach to secure remote access that enforces Zero Trust principles by providing granular access controls based on user identity, device posture, and other contextual factors. ZTNA solutions often include integrated monitoring and threat detection capabilities.

Conclusion

Monitoring, analytics, and threat detection are vital components of a Zero Trust architecture, enabling organizations to identify and respond to threats in real-time. By adopting continuous monitoring, leveraging advanced analytics, and automating threat detection and response, organizations can enhance their security posture and protect their critical assets.

As threats continue to evolve, so too must the tools and strategies used to detect and mitigate them. Emerging technologies such as XDR, deception technology, and ZTNA offer new opportunities to strengthen threat detection in a Zero Trust environment. By staying informed about these developments and continuously improving their monitoring and detection capabilities, organizations can stay one step ahead of cyber adversaries and safeguard their operations against the ever-present risk of cyberattacks.

Chapter 7

Zero Trust in Cloud Environments

7.1. Introduction to Zero Trust in Cloud Environments

As organizations increasingly migrate their workloads to the cloud, traditional security models that rely on perimeter defenses become obsolete. The cloud introduces new complexities, including shared responsibility models, dynamic environments, and the proliferation of microservices. In this context, Zero Trust has emerged as a critical framework for securing cloud environments, where the assumption is that no entity—whether inside or outside the network—can be trusted by default.

Zero Trust in the cloud emphasizes identity verification, continuous monitoring, and strict access controls for all users, devices, and applications. This approach aligns with the cloud's dynamic nature, ensuring that security policies adapt to changing conditions and that sensitive data remains protected, regardless of where it resides.

7.2. The Challenges of Cloud Security

Cloud environments present unique challenges that make traditional security approaches inadequate. These challenges include:

- **Dynamic Infrastructure:** Unlike traditional on-premises infrastructure, cloud environments are highly dynamic, with resources being spun up and down frequently. This makes it difficult to maintain consistent security policies across all assets.

- **Shared Responsibility Model:** Cloud providers and customers share security responsibilities, with providers securing the underlying infrastructure and customers securing their data and applications. This division of responsibility can lead to gaps in security if not properly managed.

- **Multi-Cloud and Hybrid Environments:** Many organizations use multiple cloud providers or a combination of on-premises and cloud resources, adding complexity to security management. Ensuring consistent security policies across diverse environments is a significant challenge.

- **Visibility and Control:** The cloud can obscure visibility into network traffic and user activities, making it difficult to detect and respond to threats. Additionally, traditional security tools may not work effectively in cloud environments, requiring new approaches to monitoring and threat detection.

- **Compliance and Data Sovereignty:** Cloud environments must comply with various regulations, such as GDPR, HIPAA, and others, depending on the industry and region. Ensuring that data remains within compliant boundaries and meets data sovereignty requirements is a complex task in the cloud.

7.3. Core Principles of Zero Trust in Cloud Environments

Implementing Zero Trust in cloud environments requires adhering to core principles that address the unique challenges of the cloud:

- **Identity-Centric Security:** In the cloud, identity becomes the primary security perimeter. Zero Trust requires robust identity verification and management practices, including multi-factor authentication (MFA), role-based access control (RBAC), and identity federation across multiple cloud platforms.

- **Least Privilege Access:** Zero Trust enforces the principle of least privilege, ensuring that users and applications have only the permissions necessary to perform their tasks. In the cloud, this means carefully managing access controls for cloud resources, APIs, and data.

- **Continuous Verification:** In a Zero Trust cloud environment, access is continuously verified based on context, such as user behavior, device health, and network conditions. This continuous verification reduces the risk of unauthorized access due to compromised credentials or other factors.

- **Micro-Segmentation:** Micro-segmentation is a key strategy in Zero Trust, involving the creation of small, isolated security zones within the cloud environment. This limits the lateral movement of attackers and contains potential breaches within specific segments of the network.

- Data Protection and Encryption:
Data security is paramount in the cloud, with Zero Trust emphasizing encryption of data at rest, in transit, and in use. Additionally, organizations must implement strong key management practices and ensure that data access is tightly controlled.

7.4. Implementing Zero Trust in Cloud Environments

Implementing Zero Trust in the cloud requires a systematic approach that aligns with the cloud's unique characteristics. Key steps include:

- Adopting a Cloud-Native Zero Trust Model: Cloud-native security solutions are designed to integrate seamlessly with cloud environments, leveraging cloud-specific features such as serverless computing, containers, and API gateways. Organizations should choose security tools and frameworks that are optimized for cloud deployments.

- Integrating Identity and Access Management (IAM) with Zero Trust: IAM solutions in the cloud must be integrated with Zero Trust principles, ensuring that access is based on verified identity and context. This includes implementing MFA, conditional access policies, and just-in-time (JIT) access to minimize exposure.

- Applying Micro-Segmentation and Network Security: Micro-segmentation in the cloud involves dividing the environment into small, manageable segments, each with its own security controls. This limits the potential impact of a breach and prevents attackers from moving laterally within the network. Cloud-native security groups, firewalls, and virtual private clouds (VPCs) are key tools for implementing micro-segmentation.

- Enhancing Visibility and Monitoring: Continuous monitoring is essential in a Zero Trust cloud environment. Organizations should deploy cloud-native security information and event management (SIEM) solutions, as well as cloud workload protection platforms (CWPPs), to gain visibility into all activities and detect anomalies in real-time.

- Automating Security Policies and Compliance: Automation is critical for maintaining security in dynamic cloud environments. Organizations should automate security policy enforcement, compliance checks, and incident response workflows to ensure that security remains consistent and effective as the cloud environment evolves.

- **Securing Cloud Data:** Data security in the cloud requires a multi-layered approach. Organizations should encrypt data at rest and in transit, implement strong access controls, and use data loss prevention (DLP) solutions to prevent unauthorized data exfiltration. Additionally, cloud providers offer native encryption and key management services that should be leveraged to protect sensitive information.

7.5. Case Studies: Zero Trust in Action in the Cloud

To illustrate the effectiveness of Zero Trust in cloud environments, consider the following case studies:

- **Case Study 1:** A Financial Institution's Transition to the Cloud: A large financial institution migrated its operations to a multi-cloud environment while implementing Zero Trust principles. By adopting a cloud-native IAM solution, the institution ensured that access to sensitive financial data was tightly controlled. Continuous monitoring and micro-segmentation allowed the institution to detect and respond to threats in real-time, while encryption and data protection measures ensured compliance with industry regulations.

- **Case Study 2:** A Healthcare Provider's Cloud Security Strategy: A healthcare provider implemented Zero Trust to secure its cloud-based electronic health records (EHR) system. The provider used cloud-native security tools to enforce MFA, monitor user activities, and apply micro-segmentation to protect patient data. By automating security policy enforcement and integrating threat intelligence, the provider was able to maintain a strong security posture while meeting HIPAA compliance requirements.

- **Case Study 3:** A Technology Company's Cloud-Native Zero Trust Model: A technology company that relies heavily on cloud services for its operations adopted a Zero Trust model to secure its cloud infrastructure. The company implemented continuous verification of user identities, applied least privilege access controls, and used micro-segmentation to isolate critical applications. The company also deployed automated security tools to enforce compliance with industry standards and respond to security incidents quickly.

7.6. Best Practices for Zero Trust in Cloud Environments

To successfully implement Zero Trust in cloud environments, organizations should follow best practices that address the unique challenges and opportunities of the cloud:

- Adopt a Holistic Approach: Zero Trust in the cloud should be part of a broader security strategy that includes identity management, data protection, and threat detection. Organizations should align their cloud security efforts with overall business objectives and regulatory requirements.

- Leverage Cloud-Native Security Tools: Cloud providers offer a range of native security tools and services designed to integrate seamlessly with their platforms. Organizations should leverage these tools to enhance security, reduce complexity, and ensure consistent policy enforcement across cloud environments.

- Implement Continuous Security Monitoring: Continuous monitoring is essential for maintaining visibility and detecting threats in real-time. Organizations should deploy cloud-native monitoring solutions that provide insights into user activities, network traffic, and data access.

- Focus on Identity and Access Management: IAM is a critical component of Zero Trust in the cloud. Organizations should implement robust IAM practices, including MFA, RBAC, and conditional access policies, to ensure that only authorized users can access sensitive resources.

- **Automate Security and Compliance:** Automation is key to maintaining security in dynamic cloud environments. Organizations should automate security policy enforcement, compliance checks, and incident response workflows to ensure that security remains consistent and effective.

7.7. The Future of Zero Trust in Cloud Environments

The adoption of Zero Trust in cloud environments is expected to grow as organizations continue to migrate to the cloud and face increasingly sophisticated cyber threats. Future developments in Zero Trust cloud security may include:

- Increased Use of AI and Machine Learning: AI and machine learning will play a larger role in automating threat detection, risk assessment, and policy enforcement in Zero Trust cloud environments. These technologies will help organizations stay ahead of evolving threats and reduce the burden on security teams.

- Integration with Emerging Cloud Technologies: As cloud technologies such as serverless computing, edge computing, and multi-cloud become more prevalent, Zero Trust principles will need to be adapted to secure these environments. Organizations will need to stay informed about new cloud technologies and adjust their security strategies accordingly.

- Greater Emphasis on Data-Centric Security: Data-centric security approaches, such as encryption and data masking, will become increasingly important in Zero Trust cloud environments. Organizations will focus on protecting data at every stage of its lifecycle, regardless of where it resides in the cloud.

Conclusion

Zero Trust is a critical framework for securing cloud environments, where traditional security models are no longer sufficient. By adopting Zero Trust principles, organizations can protect their cloud resources, ensure compliance with regulations, and reduce the risk of data breaches.

Implementing Zero Trust in the cloud requires a systematic approach that includes identity-centric security, least privilege access, continuous verification, micro-segmentation, and data protection. By leveraging cloud-native security tools, automating security policies, and following best practices, organizations can build a robust security posture that adapts to the dynamic nature of the cloud.

Chapter 8

Overcoming Implementation Challenges

The implementation of a Zero Trust Security Model, while crucial in the current threat landscape, is a complex process that requires meticulous planning, robust technology, and strong organizational commitment. Although Zero Trust offers unparalleled security benefits by eliminating implicit trust within networks, its adoption is not without challenges. These challenges include organizational resistance, technical complexities, legacy infrastructure, and balancing security with user experience.

This chapter delves into the most common implementation challenges associated with Zero Trust and provides strategies to overcome them. By understanding these obstacles and addressing them head-on, organizations can successfully transition to a Zero Trust architecture and reap its full benefits.

8.2. Organizational Resistance to Change

8.2.1. The Cultural Shift Required for Zero Trust

One of the most significant challenges in implementing Zero Trust is the cultural shift required within an organization.

Traditional security models that rely on perimeter defenses have been the standard for decades. Transitioning to Zero Trust, which assumes that threats can come from within the network and thus requires stringent internal controls, can be met with resistance from employees and even some IT teams.

To overcome this, organizations need to foster a security-first mindset across all levels of the organization. This involves:

- **Leadership Buy-In:** Ensuring that senior leadership understands and supports the Zero Trust initiative is critical. Leadership must communicate the importance of Zero Trust and the risks of not adopting it, helping to drive change from the top down.

- **Employee Education and Training:** Comprehensive training programs that educate employees on the principles of Zero Trust, the reasons for its implementation, and how it affects their daily work are essential. This training should emphasize the benefits of Zero Trust, such as enhanced security and protection of sensitive data.

- **Incremental Implementation:** Rather than a wholesale shift, organizations might find success in gradually implementing Zero Trust. Starting with high-risk areas and progressively extending Zero Trust principles across the organization can reduce resistance and allow teams to adjust to the new security model.

8.2.2. Overcoming Resistance from IT Teams

IT teams accustomed to traditional security architectures might resist Zero Trust due to perceived complexity or concerns about disrupting existing systems. Overcoming this resistance requires:

- **Clear Communication of Benefits:** IT teams should be educated on how Zero Trust can reduce the attack surface, prevent lateral movement by attackers, and offer better visibility into network traffic and user behavior.

- Involvement in Planning and Implementation: Engaging IT teams in the planning process and making them part of the decision-making helps in gaining their support. Providing them with the necessary tools, training, and resources to manage Zero Trust effectively is also crucial.

- Proof of Concept (PoC): Running a PoC for Zero Trust within a limited scope can demonstrate its effectiveness and help IT teams become familiar with its tools and processes before a full-scale rollout.

8.3. Technical Complexities

8.3.1. Integration with Legacy Systems

Many organizations operate with legacy systems that were not designed with Zero Trust in mind. These systems can be difficult to secure using Zero Trust principles due to their outdated technology and lack of compatibility with modern security tools.

To address this challenge:

- Legacy System Modernization: Where feasible, organizations should consider modernizing or replacing legacy systems that cannot be secured adequately. This may involve migrating applications to cloud-based platforms that support Zero Trust principles.

- Compensating Controls: For legacy systems that cannot be replaced, compensating controls such as enhanced monitoring, network segmentation, and strict access controls can help secure these systems within a Zero Trust framework.

- Layered Security Approach: Implementing a layered security strategy that combines traditional security measures with Zero Trust controls can help protect legacy systems during the transition period.

8.3.2. Complexity of Network Segmentation and Micro-Segmentation

Network segmentation is a cornerstone of Zero Trust, involving the division of networks into smaller, isolated segments to limit the movement of attackers. However, implementing effective network segmentation, especially micro-segmentation, can be complex and resource-intensive.

Strategies to overcome this complexity include:

- **Automated Tools:** Utilizing automation tools that can dynamically segment the network based on policy and traffic patterns can significantly reduce the complexity and workload associated with manual segmentation.

- Zero Trust Network Access (ZTNA): ZTNA solutions can provide granular access control at the application layer, reducing the need for extensive network segmentation by controlling access at a higher level.

- Start Small and Scale: Organizations should start with segmenting high-value assets or critical applications and gradually expand segmentation to other parts of the network.

8.4. Balancing Security with User Experience

8.4.1. Ensuring Usability While Implementing Stringent Security

One of the key challenges of Zero Trust is balancing strong security controls with the need for a seamless user experience. Overly restrictive access controls, frequent multi-factor authentication (MFA) prompts, and delays caused by security checks can frustrate users and reduce productivity.

To balance security with usability:

- **Adaptive Authentication:** Implementing adaptive or risk-based authentication, where the level of security checks is adjusted based on the context of the access request (e.g., location, device, behavior), can enhance security without overly burdening users.

- **Single Sign-On (SSO):** SSO solutions can reduce the friction of multiple login prompts by allowing users to authenticate once and gain access to multiple resources, all while maintaining a Zero Trust stance.

- **User-Centric Design:** Involving end-users in the design and testing of security controls can help ensure that security measures are both effective and user-friendly.

8.4.2. Educating Users About the Importance of Security

Educating users about the importance of security and their role in maintaining a secure environment is crucial. When users understand why certain security measures are in place, they are more likely to comply and less likely to feel frustrated by them.

Effective education strategies include:

- **Ongoing Security Awareness Programs:** Regular training sessions, phishing simulations, and security newsletters can keep security top of mind for employees and reinforce the importance of Zero Trust principles.

- Feedback Mechanisms: Providing users with a way to give feedback on security measures allows the organization to address concerns and improve the user experience.

8.5. Cost and Resource Constraints

8.5.1. Financial Investment in Zero Trust Technologies

Implementing Zero Trust requires investment in new technologies, such as identity and access management (IAM) systems, multi-factor authentication

(MFA), and advanced monitoring tools. For some organizations, the cost of these technologies can be a significant barrier.

To overcome financial challenges:

- **Prioritize Investments:** Organizations should prioritize investments in technologies that address the most critical security gaps. This might involve focusing on protecting high-value assets or implementing Zero Trust in the most vulnerable parts of the network first.

- **Leverage Existing Infrastructure:** Where possible, organizations should seek to leverage existing technologies and infrastructure that can be integrated into a Zero Trust framework. For example, existing IAM or SIEM systems might be enhanced with additional Zero Trust features rather than replaced.

-   **Cloud-Based Solutions:** Cloud-based security solutions, which often operate on a subscription model, can reduce upfront costs and provide flexible, scalable options for implementing Zero Trust.

8.5.2. Resource Allocation and Skill Gaps

Implementing Zero Trust requires not only financial investment but also skilled personnel who understand the complexities of modern security architectures. Many organizations face challenges in finding and retaining cybersecurity professionals with the necessary expertise.

Strategies to address resource and skill gaps include:

- **Training and Upskilling:** Investing in the training and development of existing IT staff can help bridge skill gaps. Certifications in Zero Trust, cloud security, and network segmentation can equip teams with the knowledge needed to implement and manage Zero Trust environments.

- **Managed Security Services:** For organizations with limited in-house resources, partnering with managed security service providers (MSSPs) can provide access to Zero Trust expertise without the need to hire additional full-time staff.

- Automated and AI-Driven Solutions: Leveraging AI and machine learning-driven security tools can help organizations manage Zero Trust implementations more efficiently, reducing the need for manual intervention and minimizing the impact of skill gaps.

8.6. Regulatory Compliance and Data Privacy

8.6.1. Navigating Complex Regulatory Environments

Compliance with regulations such as GDPR, HIPAA, and others adds another layer of complexity to Zero Trust implementations. Organizations must ensure that their Zero Trust initiatives align with applicable legal requirements, particularly regarding data privacy and protection.

To overcome regulatory challenges:

- Integrate Compliance into Zero Trust Planning: Organizations should incorporate regulatory requirements into their Zero Trust planning from the outset. This ensures that security controls meet both organizational and legal obligations.

- Use Compliance-Friendly Tools: Choosing Zero Trust tools and solutions that are designed with regulatory compliance in mind can simplify the process of meeting legal requirements. Many cloud-based security solutions offer built-in compliance features that help organizations stay within legal boundaries.

- Regular Audits and Assessments: Conducting regular audits and assessments of the Zero Trust environment ensures that compliance is maintained as regulations evolve and the organization's security posture changes.

8.6.2. Data Privacy Considerations

Zero Trust emphasizes continuous monitoring and data collection to identify and respond to threats. However, this increased visibility can raise concerns about data privacy, especially in regions with strict privacy laws.

To address data privacy concerns:

- Data Minimization: Collect only the data necessary for security purposes and ensure that monitoring tools are configured to avoid unnecessary collection of personal information.

- Anonymization and Encryption: Where possible, anonymize or encrypt sensitive data to protect it from unauthorized access, even within the organization.

- Transparency with Users: Clearly communicate to users what data is being collected, how it is used, and the measures in place to protect their privacy. Transparency builds trust and can alleviate concerns about monitoring and data collection.

8.7. Future-Proofing Zero Trust Implementations

8.7.1. Adapting to Evolving Threats

The cybersecurity landscape is continuously evolving, with new threats emerging regularly. As a result, Zero Trust implementations must be designed to adapt and respond to these changes effectively. To future-proof Zero Trust strategies:

- Continuous Threat Intelligence: Implementing a robust threat intelligence program that continuously monitors for new and emerging threats is crucial. This includes integrating threat feeds, analyzing security incidents, and staying informed about vulnerabilities and exploits relevant to your environment.

- Regularly Updating Security Controls: Security controls and policies should be regularly reviewed and updated to address new threats and vulnerabilities. This includes updating access controls, refining network segmentation, and revisiting encryption standards as needed.

- Agility in Incident Response: Ensuring that the incident response plan is agile and can quickly adapt to different types of security incidents is essential. This may involve using automated tools to detect and respond to threats in real-time and conducting regular incident response drills to prepare for various scenarios.

8.7.2. Leveraging Automation and Artificial Intelligence

Automation and AI play a critical role in the future of Zero Trust, enabling organizations to manage complex environments with greater efficiency and effectiveness. By leveraging these technologies:

- **Automated Policy Enforcement:** Automation can ensure that security policies are consistently applied across the entire organization. This includes automated identity verification, access control, and network segmentation, reducing the risk of human error and enhancing security.

- AI-Powered Threat Detection: AI can analyze vast amounts of data to identify patterns and anomalies that may indicate a security breach. Machine learning algorithms can continuously improve by learning from past incidents, making AI-powered systems increasingly effective at detecting and responding to threats.

- Predictive Analytics: AI can also be used for predictive analytics, identifying potential threats before they materialize. By analyzing historical data, AI can forecast where and how an attack might occur, allowing organizations to proactively strengthen their defenses.

8.8. Case Studies: Overcoming Challenges in Real-World Implementations

Examining real-world case studies provides valuable insights into how organizations have successfully overcome challenges in Zero Trust implementation. These case studies highlight different industries, organizational sizes, and unique challenges:

- **Case Study 1:** A Financial Institution's Transition to Zero Trust: This case study explores how a large financial institution overcame the challenge of integrating Zero Trust with its legacy systems. By adopting a phased approach, starting with high-risk areas, and leveraging compensating controls, the institution successfully secured its environment without disrupting operations.

- **Case Study 2:** A Healthcare Provider's Balancing Act: A healthcare provider faced the challenge of balancing strict security measures with the need for seamless access to patient data. The organization implemented adaptive authentication and a user-centric design approach, ensuring that security did not hinder the delivery of critical healthcare services.

- **Case Study 3:** A Global Manufacturer's Zero Trust Rollout: A global manufacturer with a complex, multi-national IT environment overcame the challenge of cultural resistance by involving its IT teams in every step of the Zero Trust implementation process. The company used a proof-of-concept approach, demonstrating the effectiveness of Zero Trust and gaining buy-in from all stakeholders.

Conclusion

Overcoming the challenges associated with Zero Trust implementation requires a strategic approach that addresses both technical and organizational obstacles. By fostering a security-first culture, leveraging automation and AI, and continuously adapting to new threats, organizations can successfully implement Zero Trust and build a robust security posture for the future.

This chapter has outlined the primary challenges of Zero Trust adoption, offering practical strategies to mitigate them. By applying these insights, organizations can navigate the complexities of Zero Trust, ensuring that they protect their critical assets, comply with regulatory requirements, and maintain a secure and resilient environment in an ever-changing threat landscape.

Chapter 9

Future Trends and Innovations in Zero Trust

Zero Trust is more than just a security framework; it represents a paradigm shift in how organizations think about cybersecurity. As the threat landscape continues to evolve, so too must the principles and technologies underpinning Zero Trust. This chapter explores the future trends and innovations that are likely to shape the Zero Trust Security Model in the coming years. From the integration of advanced technologies like artificial intelligence (AI) and machine learning (ML) to the increasing importance of securing edge computing and IoT devices, this chapter will provide a comprehensive look at where Zero Trust is heading and how organizations can prepare for these changes.

9.2. AI and Machine Learning in Zero Trust

9.2.1. Enhancing Threat Detection and Response

Artificial intelligence and machine learning are poised to play a critical role in the future of Zero Trust. These technologies can enhance threat detection and response capabilities by analyzing vast amounts of data, identifying patterns, and detecting anomalies that might indicate a security breach. Unlike traditional rule-based systems, AI and ML can learn from historical data, improving their accuracy and reducing false positives over time.

- **Automated Decision-Making:** AI-driven systems can automate the decision-making process, dynamically adjusting security policies based on real-time data. For example, if an AI system detects unusual behavior from a user or device, it can automatically restrict access or require additional authentication before granting access to sensitive resources.

- **Predictive Analytics:** ML algorithms can predict potential security incidents by analyzing trends and patterns in data. This predictive capability allows organizations to proactively address vulnerabilities before they can be exploited by attackers.

9.2.2. Reducing the Complexity of Zero Trust Implementation

One of the challenges of implementing Zero Trust is its complexity, especially in large, distributed environments. AI and ML can help reduce this complexity by automating many of the tasks associated with Zero Trust, such as identity verification, access control, and network segmentation. By leveraging AI, organizations can streamline their Zero

Trust deployments, making it easier to scale and manage these environments.

9.3. Integration with Edge Computing and IoT

9.3.1. Securing the Edge

As organizations increasingly adopt edge computing to process data closer to where it is generated, the need for Zero Trust at the edge becomes paramount. Traditional security models are not well-suited for edge environments, where data is processed outside the traditional corporate perimeter. Zero Trust, with its emphasis on continuous verification and least privilege access, is ideally suited for securing edge computing environments.

- Decentralized Security Models: In edge environments, security must be decentralized, with each edge device or micro-data center enforcing Zero Trust principles. This requires lightweight, scalable security solutions that can operate efficiently in resource-constrained environments.

- AI-Driven Edge Security: AI and ML can be integrated into edge devices to provide real-time threat detection and response. These technologies can analyze data locally, reducing the need to send data back to a central location for analysis and enabling faster, more efficient security responses.

9.3.2. Zero Trust for IoT Devices

The proliferation of Internet of Things (IoT) devices presents a significant security challenge. IoT devices often lack robust security features, making them vulnerable to attacks. Zero Trust can help mitigate these risks by ensuring that IoT devices are authenticated, monitored, and granted access based on strict policies.

- **Micro-Segmentation for IoT:** Implementing micro-segmentation in IoT environments can prevent compromised devices from being used as a foothold to launch attacks on the broader network. By isolating IoT devices into separate network segments, organizations can limit the potential damage caused by a security breach.

- **Device Authentication and Encryption:** Zero Trust requires that every IoT device be authenticated before it is granted access to the network. Additionally, data transmitted by IoT devices should be encrypted to protect against interception and tampering.

9.4. The Role of Blockchain in Zero Trust

9.4.1. Decentralized Identity Management

Blockchain technology has the potential to revolutionize identity management within a Zero Trust framework. Traditional identity management systems rely on centralized authorities, which can become single points of failure. Blockchain, with its decentralized and immutable ledger, can provide a more secure and resilient approach to managing identities.

- **Self-Sovereign Identity:** Blockchain enables self-sovereign identity, where individuals and organizations have control over their digital identities without relying on a central authority. In a Zero Trust environment, this allows for more secure and private authentication processes.

- Tamper-Proof Audit Trails: Blockchain can also provide tamper-proof audit trails for authentication and access events. This ensures that all actions within a Zero Trust environment are recorded in an immutable ledger, providing a reliable source of truth for compliance and forensic investigations.

9.4.2. Smart Contracts for Access Control

Smart contracts, which are self-executing contracts with the terms of the agreement directly written into code, can be used to enforce access control policies in a Zero Trust environment. For example, a smart contract could automatically grant or revoke access based on predefined conditions, such as the user's role, time of access, or location.

- **Automated Compliance Enforcement:** Smart contracts can also be used to enforce compliance with security policies automatically. If a user or device violates a security policy, the smart contract can immediately revoke access or trigger other security measures, ensuring that compliance is maintained at all times.

9.5. Quantum-Resistant Cryptography

9.5.1. The Threat of Quantum Computing

Quantum computing poses a significant threat to traditional cryptographic algorithms. As quantum computers become more powerful, they could potentially break encryption methods that are currently considered secure. This presents a challenge for Zero Trust environments, which rely heavily on encryption to protect data and communications.

- Quantum-Resistant Algorithms: To future-proof Zero Trust environments, organizations must begin adopting quantum-resistant cryptographic algorithms. These algorithms are designed to withstand the computational power of quantum computers, ensuring that encrypted data remains secure even in a post-quantum world.

- **Hybrid Cryptographic Approaches:** In the near term, organizations may adopt hybrid cryptographic approaches that combine traditional and quantum-resistant algorithms. This provides an additional layer of security while the industry transitions to fully quantum-resistant solutions.

9.5.2. Preparing for the Quantum Era

Preparing for the quantum era requires organizations to start assessing their cryptographic infrastructure and planning for the transition to quantum-resistant algorithms. This involves identifying which systems and data are most at risk and prioritizing their protection.

- **Long-Term Data Security:** Organizations must consider the long-term security of their data. Even if quantum computers are not yet capable of breaking current encryption, data that is encrypted today could be vulnerable in the future if it is stored long enough.

Transitioning to quantum-resistant cryptography now can help protect sensitive data for the long term.

9.6. Zero Trust and Regulatory Compliance

9.6.1. Adapting to New Regulations

As governments and regulatory bodies continue to develop new cybersecurity regulations, Zero Trust will need to adapt to ensure compliance. This includes not only adhering to current regulations but also being flexible enough to meet future requirements.

- Privacy-First Security Models: As data privacy becomes an increasingly important concern, Zero Trust must evolve to prioritize privacy alongside security. This includes implementing strong data protection measures and ensuring that security practices do not infringe on individuals' privacy rights.

- Compliance Automation: To reduce the burden of regulatory compliance, organizations may increasingly turn to automation. Automated compliance tools can monitor and enforce adherence to regulations, reducing the risk of human error and ensuring that organizations remain compliant in real time.

9.6.2. Zero Trust in Global Contexts

Different regions have varying cybersecurity regulations and standards. As organizations operate in an increasingly global context, Zero Trust implementations must be adaptable to meet the requirements of different jurisdictions.

- **Cross-Border Data Flows:** Zero Trust must address the challenges of cross-border data flows, ensuring that data is protected in transit and at rest, regardless of where it is located. This includes complying with regulations such as the GDPR, which imposes strict requirements on the transfer of data across borders.

- **Localized Security Practices:** Organizations may need to tailor their Zero Trust practices to meet local regulatory requirements. This could involve adapting encryption standards, data retention policies, and access controls to comply with regional laws and regulations.

9.7. The Evolution of Zero Trust Architecture

9.7.1. Moving Beyond Network Security

While Zero Trust initially focused on network security, its principles are increasingly being applied to other areas of cybersecurity. This includes extending Zero Trust to application security, endpoint security, and even physical security.

- Zero Trust for Applications: As applications become more complex and distributed, Zero Trust principles are being applied to secure the application layer. This involves ensuring that applications are developed with security in mind, and that access to application data and functionality is tightly controlled.

- Endpoint Security and Zero Trust: With the rise of remote work and mobile devices, endpoint security has become a critical component of Zero Trust. This includes enforcing strict access controls on devices, continuously monitoring device health, and ensuring that endpoints are regularly updated and patched.

9.7.2. Zero Trust for Physical Security

The concept of Zero Trust is also being extended to physical security, particularly in environments where digital and physical security intersect, such as smart buildings and critical infrastructure.

- **Integrating Digital and Physical Security:** In smart buildings, Zero Trust principles can be applied to control access to physical spaces, ensuring that only authorized individuals can enter sensitive areas. This involves integrating physical access controls with digital identity and access management systems.

- **Protecting Critical Infrastructure:** In critical infrastructure environments, such as power plants and transportation systems, Zero Trust can help protect against both cyber and physical threats. This includes implementing strong authentication and access controls for both digital systems and physical facilities.

Conclusion

The future of Zero Trust is marked by significant innovation and evolution as it adapts to emerging technologies, threats, and regulatory landscapes. The integration of AI, machine learning, blockchain, and quantum-resistant cryptography represents the next frontier in cybersecurity, enabling organizations to implement Zero Trust in ways that were previously unimaginable. The focus on securing edge computing, IoT devices, and even physical security systems highlights

Zero Trust's growing relevance in an increasingly interconnected world.

As organizations look to the future, they must recognize that Zero Trust is not a one-time initiative but an ongoing journey. The principles of Zero Trust must be continuously revisited, refined, and expanded to address the ever-changing threat landscape and technological advancements. By staying ahead of these trends and embracing the innovations outlined in this chapter, organizations can ensure that their Zero Trust architectures remain robust, resilient, and capable of protecting their most critical assets in the years to come.

This chapter concludes with a reminder that the key to successfully implementing and maintaining a Zero Trust environment lies in continuous learning, adaptability, and the willingness to embrace new technologies and methodologies. The organizations that thrive in the future will be those that view Zero Trust not just as a security model but as a strategic enabler for innovation, growth, and resilience in an increasingly digital and interconnected world.

Chapter 10

Case Studies and Practical Applications

In the realm of cybersecurity, theory must meet practice to be truly effective. The Zero Trust Security Model, with its emphasis on "never trust, always verify," has proven to be a powerful framework for protecting sensitive data and systems. However, its successful implementation requires more than just understanding the underlying principles; it demands practical application in real-world environments. This chapter presents a series of detailed case studies and practical applications, demonstrating how organizations across various industries have successfully adopted Zero Trust to address their unique security challenges. By exploring these examples, readers will gain insights into the practical aspects of Zero Trust implementation, the challenges encountered, and the innovative solutions employed to overcome them.

Case Study 1: Financial Sector - Protecting Sensitive Data

financial sector is one of the most heavily targeted industries by cybercriminals, given the sensitive nature of the data it handles. A large multinational bank, facing increasing regulatory pressure and sophisticated cyber threats, decided to transition to a Zero Trust architecture to enhance its security posture.

Implementation Strategy

The bank's Zero Trust journey began with a comprehensive assessment of its existing security infrastructure. Key steps in the implementation included:

- **Network Segmentation:** The bank implemented micro-segmentation across its networks to ensure that access to sensitive financial data was restricted to only those who required it for their job functions. This involved creating secure zones within the network, each governed by strict access control policies.

- **Multi-Factor Authentication (MFA):** To strengthen identity and access management, the bank rolled out MFA across all critical systems. This ensured that even if credentials were compromised, unauthorized access would still be thwarted by an additional layer of verification.

- **Continuous Monitoring and Analytics:** The bank adopted advanced monitoring tools that provided real-time visibility into user and device activity. This allowed for the immediate detection of suspicious behavior and automated responses to potential threats.

Challenges Encountered

The primary challenge faced by the bank was the integration of Zero Trust with its legacy systems. Many of these systems were not designed with Zero Trust in mind and required significant modifications to comply with the new security policies. Additionally, there was resistance from employees who found the new security measures cumbersome.

Outcomes**

Despite these challenges, the bank successfully reduced the risk of data breaches and improved its overall security posture. The Zero Trust architecture provided better control over who could access sensitive financial data, leading to greater regulatory compliance and enhanced customer trust. Moreover, the bank reported a significant reduction in security incidents, with many potential threats being neutralized before they could cause damage.

Case Study 2: Healthcare Sector - Securing Patient Data**

A regional healthcare provider sought to protect patient data amidst rising threats from ransomware and other cyberattacks. The healthcare provider was also required to comply with stringent regulations such as the Health Insurance Portability and Accountability Act (HIPAA), which mandates the protection of patient information.

Implementation Strategy

The healthcare provider implemented Zero Trust with a focus on protecting electronic health records (EHRs) and ensuring secure access to patient data across its network of hospitals and clinics. Key initiatives included:

-     **Identity and Access Management (IAM):** The provider introduced a robust IAM system that ensured only authorized personnel could access patient data. This system was integrated with the provider's existing electronic health record (EHR) platform, providing seamless and secure access.

- **Data Encryption:** All patient data, both at rest and in transit, was encrypted using industry-standard encryption protocols. This ensured that even if data were intercepted, it would be unreadable without the appropriate decryption keys.

- **Zero Trust Network Access (ZTNA):** The provider implemented ZTNA to secure remote access to its network, particularly important during the COVID-19 pandemic when many healthcare workers were operating remotely. ZTNA provided secure, policy-based access to specific applications, reducing the attack surface.

Challenges Encountered

One of the major challenges was the need for rapid implementation during the COVID-19 pandemic when the provider was also dealing with the pressures of the public health crisis. Additionally, ensuring compliance with HIPAA while implementing Zero Trust required careful coordination between the IT and legal teams.

Outcomes

The implementation of Zero Trust led to a marked improvement in the provider's security posture. The encryption of patient data and the implementation of IAM and ZTNA significantly reduced the risk of data breaches. The provider also achieved full compliance with HIPAA, avoiding potential fines and penalties. The healthcare staff adapted to the new security measures with minimal disruption to their workflow, ensuring that patient care remained a top priority.

Case Study 3: Technology Sector - Safeguarding Intellectual Property**

A leading technology company, known for its innovation in software development, faced the challenge of protecting its intellectual property (IP) from cyber espionage. The company decided to adopt a Zero Trust architecture to safeguard its sensitive research and development (R&D) data.

Implementation Strategy

The company's Zero Trust strategy focused on securing its development environment and preventing unauthorized access to its IP. The implementation included:

- **Micro-Segmentation and Access Controls:** The company

implemented micro-segmentation within its network to isolate its R&D environment from the rest of the corporate network. Access controls were strictly enforced, with only authorized personnel allowed access to specific segments based on their roles.

- **Advanced Threat Detection:** The company deployed advanced threat detection systems powered by artificial intelligence (AI) and machine learning (ML). These systems continuously monitored the network for unusual activity, such as unauthorized access attempts or data exfiltration.

- **Zero Trust for DevOps:** To secure the software development lifecycle, the company integrated Zero Trust principles into its DevOps practices. This included secure coding practices, continuous security testing, and automated security policy enforcement throughout the development process.

Challenges Encountered

A significant challenge was the need to balance security with the fast-paced, collaborative nature of software development. Developers were initially resistant to the security controls, viewing them as impediments to productivity. Additionally, integrating Zero Trust with existing DevOps tools and processes required careful planning and coordination.

Outcomes**

The Zero Trust implementation successfully protected the company's IP from potential cyber threats. The advanced threat detection systems provided early warnings of attempted intrusions, allowing the security team to respond swiftly. Over time, the company was able to integrate security into its DevOps culture, with developers embracing the importance of secure coding practices. The company reported no major security incidents post-implementation, demonstrating the effectiveness of its Zero Trust strategy.

Practical Applications of Zero Trust in Emerging Technologies**

Zero Trust in Cloud Computing**

As organizations continue to migrate to cloud environments, applying Zero Trust principles in the cloud becomes increasingly important. Practical applications of Zero Trust in cloud computing include:

- **Cloud Access Security Brokers (CASBs):** CASBs act as intermediaries between users and cloud service providers, enforcing security policies such as encryption, access control, and data loss prevention. They are crucial for implementing Zero Trust in multi-cloud environments.

- **Zero Trust Network Access (ZTNA) in the Cloud:** ZTNA solutions provide secure, policy-based access to cloud applications and services, ensuring that users are only granted access to the resources they need, regardless of their location.

- **Securing Serverless Architectures:** In serverless computing, where code is executed in response to events, Zero Trust can be applied by ensuring that each function invocation is authenticated and authorized, and that data is encrypted both in transit and at rest.

Zero Trust for Internet of Things (IoT)**

The proliferation of IoT devices presents unique security challenges that can be addressed through Zero Trust:

\-   ****Device Identity and Authentication:**** Zero Trust requires that every IoT device be uniquely identified and authenticated before being granted access to the network. This prevents unauthorized devices from connecting and potentially compromising the system.

- **Micro-Segmentation of IoT Networks:** IoT devices should be segmented into different network zones based on their function and risk profile. This limits the impact of a compromised device and prevents lateral movement across the network.

- **Endpoint Security for IoT:** Zero Trust principles can be applied to IoT endpoints, ensuring that devices are regularly updated with security patches and monitored for signs of compromise.

Conclusion

The case studies and practical applications discussed in this chapter illustrate the versatility and effectiveness of the Zero Trust Security Model across different industries and technological environments. Whether protecting financial data, securing patient information, or safeguarding intellectual property, Zero Trust provides a robust framework for addressing today's cybersecurity challenges.

As more organizations embrace digital transformation, the practical application of Zero Trust will continue to evolve, adapting to new threats and integrating with emerging technologies. By learning from the experiences of others and applying these principles to their own environments, organizations can build more secure, resilient infrastructures capable of withstanding the ever-changing landscape of cyber threats.

This chapter serves as a comprehensive guide to understanding how Zero Trust can be practically implemented and the real-world benefits it can deliver. It underscores the importance of a proactive approach to cybersecurity, where trust is never assumed, and security is continuously enforced.